NOODLES COOKBOOK

A Complete Cookbook of Asian Noodle Dish Ideas!

(Happiness Is When You Have a Noodle Cookbook!)

Venita Hagler

Published by Alex Howard

© **Venita Hagler**

All Rights Reserved

Noodles Cookbook: A Complete Cookbook of Asian Noodle Dish Ideas!
(Happiness Is When You Have a Noodle Cookbook!)

ISBN 978-1-990169-78-6

All rights reserved. No part of this guide may be reproduced in any form without permission in writing from the publisher except in the case of brief quotations embodied in critical articles or reviews.

Legal & Disclaimer

The information contained in this book is not designed to replace or take the place of any form of medicine or professional medical advice. The information in this book has been provided for educational and entertainment purposes only.

The information contained in this book has been compiled from sources deemed reliable, and it is accurate to the best of the Author's knowledge; however, the Author cannot guarantee its accuracy and validity and cannot be held liable for any errors or omissions. Changes are periodically made to this book. You must consult your doctor or get professional medical advice before using any of the suggested remedies, techniques, or information in this book.

Table of contents

Part 1 1
Introduction 2
1. Veg Chow Mein Noodles 3
2. Schezwan Noodles Recipe 5
3. Chinese Egg Noodles 7
4. Crispy Chinese Noodle Egg Rolls 9
5. Maggi Noodles Spring Roll 11
6. Chapati Noodles 13
7. Maggi Pakoda 15
8. Cheesy Maggi Noodles Bread Pockets 17
9. Cheesy Maggi Bread Rolls 19
10. Maggi Noodle Momos Recipe 21
11. Vegetable Hakka Noodles 23
12. Noodles Spring Rolls 25
13. Pad Thai Noodles 28
14. Chili Garlic Noodles 30
15. Chicken Stir-Fry Noodles 31
16. Bread Rolls With Noodles Stuffing 33
17. Shrimp And Vegetable Stir Fry Noodles 35
18. Left-Over Roti Noodles 37
19. Singapore Noodles 39
20. Singapore Rice Noodle 41
21. Hong Kong Style Wonton Noodle Soup 43
22. Classic Singapore Noodles 45
23. Quick Peanut Butter Noodles 47

24. Mie Goreng Indonesian Stir-Fried Noodles 49
25. Chinese Hand Pulled Noodles 51
26. Noodles Samosa 52
27. Vegetable And Noodle Soup 56
28. Vegetable Noodles 57
29. Chicken Hakka Noodles Recipe 58
30. Chicken Chow Mein Recipe 61
31. Japchae (Glass Noodles Stir-Fried With Vegetables) 63
32. Maggi/Ramen Masala Recipe 67
33. Maggi Noodles Spring Roll 69
34. Noodles Tava Cutlet 71
35. Triple Schezwan Noodles 73
36. Shanghai Stewed Noodles 75
37. Thukpa - Tibetan Noodle Soup 76
38. Korean Ramyeon 79
39. Korean Noodle Soup 81
40. Quick Ramen Noodle Soup 84
41. Schezwan Paneer Noodles 85
42. Paneer Noodles 87
43. Paneer Maggi Noodles 88
44. Crispy Paneer Noodle Fries 90
45. Stir Fry Noodles With Vegetables With Fried Tofu 91
46. Udon Noodle Soup 94
47. Beef Udon 95
48. Chinese Beef Noodle Soup 98
49. Beef Teriyaki Noodles 100
50. Uzbek Lagman 102

Part 2	104
Introduction	105
Veggie Butternut Squash Noodles With Brown Butter, Sage And Pumpkin Seed Pesto	106
Veggie Zucchini Noodles Plus Pancetta And Parmesan	108
Veggie Noodle With Avocado, Tomato And Pine Nut Courgetti	110
Veggie Paleo Celeriac Carbonara Casserole	112
Veggie Noodle Curry Butternut Squash	115
Veggie Rainbow Noodle Salad	118
Veggie Chive Oil Zucchini Noodles With Roasted Tofu	119
Veggie Noodle Sauteed Zucchini Ribbions	121
Veggie Noodle With Sweet Potato And Spicy Pepita Gremolata	122
Veggie Noodles One-Pot Healthy Pasta	124
Veggie Noodle Teriyaki Chicken	125
Veggie Noodles With Spinach, Bacon, Mushroom And Sweet Potato	127
Noodle Recipes	129
1) Soba Noodle Soup	129
2) Chanpon Noodles	131
3) Hakata Ramen	134
4) Miso Ramen	136
5) Coconut Lime Noodle Soup	139
6) Shrimp Noodle Soup	141
7) Udon Miso Noodle Soup	143
8) Sweet Red Chili Noodles With Sesame Seeds	145
9) Tsuke-Men Noodles	146

10) Sirloin-Snap Pea Stir-Fry 148
11) Fried Ramen Soup 149
12) Sapporo Ramen 150
13) Tan Tan Ramen Noodles 154
14) Yakisoba Noodle Stir Fry 157
15) Sesame Ramen Noodles 159
16) Hiyashi Chuka 160
17) Sesame-Crusted Tuna With Ponzu Glaze On Ramen Noodles 162
18) Abura Soba Noodles 164
19) Ramen Noodle Salad With Zucchini And Carrots 166
20) Ramen And Cheese 168
21) Ramen Noodles With Wild Mushrooms And Parmesan Sauce 169
22) Tom Yum Noodle Soup 171
23) Salmon In Parchment 173
24) Ramepherd's Pie 175
25) Stir-Fry Ramen With Peppers And Shrimp 177
26) Crunchy Ramen Snack Mix 178
27) Ramen Burger 180
28) Salmon Cakes With Creamy Tomato-Garlic Sauce 182
29) Ramen Crust Pizza 185
30) Ramen-Crusted Fried Chicken 186
Healthy Ramen Noodles 188
Sweet Potato Ramen 188
Hot Garlic Ramen 189

Part 1

Introduction

Best Sandwich Recipes book is a Product of Authentic CookBooks. Republishing for Commercial or selling this book in any form is Prohibited without consulting Authentic CookBooks. All Rights Reserved.

You can use this book Recipes for Learning Purpose and making Recipes for Your Loved Ones, Friends, Guest and also for Your Restraunts and Hotels.

Learn and recreate Beautiful Recipes.

We have other Recipes Ebooks also,Please Checkout!!!

1. Veg Chow Mein Noodles

Ingredients –

Noodles 50gm

Butter 3 spoons

White pepper masala (spice) 1 spoon

Ajinomoto 1 spoon

Salt

Tomato ketchup

Carrot (gajar) 1 only

Cabbage (patta Gobi) 50gm

Beans

Capsicum

Onion 1 (pyaz)

Soya sauce (ketchup)

Chili sauce (ketchup)

Direction

1. Take a deep pan add water and getting warm put noodles on the water.

2. Water is boiled now and stirs well and cooks for 4-5 min.

3. Now separate water and noodles, drain all water.

4. Now quickly rinse cold water for stopping cook the noodles.

5. Take a pan and heat, add in butter.

6. Now add in pan onion stir it high flame till it gets transparent.

7. Now add in all veggies, stir well.

8. Now we will add spices it.

9. Add salt to taste, add 1tsp white pepper, add some Ajinomoto and mix well.

10. Stir for 3-4 mins and now we will put noodles in the pan.

11. Now add soy sauce, add chili sauce, and stir well.

12. Now add ketchup and mix well 3-4 min.

13. Now noodles are ready, garnish it with coriander leaves.

2.Schezwan Noodles Recipe

Ingredients:

1 cup Boiled Noodles

1 tsp Sesame oil

1 tbsp Garlic

1/2 tbsp Ginger

Sliced Carrot

Sliced Onion

Sliced Green Pepper

Sliced Cabbage

1 1/2 tsp Tomato sauce

1/2 tsp Soya sauce

1 tsp Schezwan sauce

1/2 tsp Vinegar

1/2 tsp Black pepper powder

Salt to taste

Spring Onion for garnishing

Direction –

- Heat up a pan on high heat. Add sesame oil.
- You can use regular cooking oil instead of sesame oil.
- When the oil is enough hot, add garlic and ginger. Fry for just about 30 seconds.

- Add carrot, onion green pepper. Mix well and fry for just about a minute.
- Veggies should retain its crunch.
- Add sliced cabbage and mix well. No need to cook.
- Add tomato sauce, soya sauce, schezwan sauce, vinegar, black pepper powder and salt to taste.
- Mix everything well together.
- Add boiled noodles. Boil noodles according to packet instructions.
- Mix well with the help of the pair of tongs. Fry noodles on high heat for about 5-6 minutes.
- Add spring onion and schezwan noodles are already.
- You can have these as it is.
- These go well with Gobi Manchurian.

3.Chinese Egg Noodles

Ingredients –

Plain noodles 250gm

Green bell pepper 1

Eggs 3

Cabbage chopped 1 cup

Dark soy sauce 1tbsp

White vinegar 1 tbsp

Red chili powder ½ tsp

Black pepper powder ½ or ¼ tsp

Oil 4 tbsp

Salt ½ or ¼ tsp

Direction –

1. Cooking for noodles –take a deep pan add water and bring it to boil.
2. When the water boil to add salt so the water taste salty.
3. Add a little oil so the noodles will not stick.
4. Add plain noodles to the boiling water and cook for 3-4 mins.
5. Turn off the heat and strain out the water from noodles immediately.
6. Keep noodles under running water in a strainer.
7. It stops noodles from the further cooking.
8. Now heat a pan, add 4 tbsp oil.

9. When the oil hot, break eggs into wok directly.

10. When they start to set like an omelet, start scrambling them.

11. After scrambling eggs, add sliced cabbage, capsicum and sauté for 2 min.

12. Add salt, red chilly powder, black pepper powder and mix well.

13. Add dark soy sauce, white vinegar and mix again.

14. Now add boiled noodles, mix well carefully and cook high flame for 2-3 mins until all the ingredients are mixed well.

15. Turn off the heat and serve hot.

Note –do not over boil the noodles.

4. Crispy Chinese Noodle Egg Rolls

Ingredients: -

For Egg-roll Batter -

1 -- cup: All-Purpose Flour

1 -- cup: Fresh Milk

2 -- eggs

2 -- tbs: Thick Cream

¼ - tsp: Salt (or) to taste

For Sealing Batter: -

½ - cup: Water

2 -- tbs: Corn flour

For Coating Batter:

1 -- egg

½ - cup: Bread Crumbs

For Stuffing: cup: Egg Noodles With Mix Vegetables

For Frying: -Cooking oil (for shallow fry)

Direction –

1. Firstly we beat the eggs.

2. Take a blender or grinder and put in milk and egg, salt, add crème, add all-purpose flour and grind it well.

3. Take a pan and heat it and drop some oil and that oil spread by tissue paper.

4. Now put on the better and slowly spread around it pan.

5. Cook on low flame and turn it another side and cook it.

6. Now pancake is ready.

7. Now take a bowl and add water and corn flour, mix it.

8. Take a plate and put them pancake, and spread some noodles on the pancake and turn to one side and coating some corn flour mix (for stick), next side put on it and again corn flour mix and again fold like a box or square shape. and leave it few min.

9. For egg roll coating- now dip the roll in egg then coated with bread crumbs.

10. Now leave the roll for ½ hr in a fridge.

11. Then take a pan and heat oil and deep fry the roll.

12. Now tasty rolls are ready to serve hot and ENJOY it.

5.Maggi Noodles Spring Roll

Ingredients -

1/4 cup shredded cabbage

1/2 capsicum cut lengthwise

1 spring onion cut lengthwise

4-5 French beans cross cut

Maggi noodles and taste maker

1 cup of tomato sauce

1 tablespoon oil

1/2 teaspoon ginger chili paste

1 teaspoon chaat masala

Salt to taste

Tabasco or capsico sauce

plain flour paste

Direction –

1. To make the filling –take pan Heat 1 tbsp oil. Sauté capsicum and

French beans for 2 minutes.

2. Now add Maggi noodles.

3. Add water and let the mixture boil.

4. Add the tastemaker.

5. Add ginger chili paste, add chaat masala, 1 and 1/2 tbsp. tomato ketchup, chopped cabbage, and spring onions.

6. Add salt as per taste and mix well.
7. To make the rolls - Take one spring roll sheet.
8. Spread the noodles mixture over the sheets.
9. Make tight rolls covering up the noodle mixture completely.
10. Fix the edges of the rolls with plain flour paste and deep fry the rolls.
11. Cut the rolls in pieces once they cool down a bit.
12. Serve with capsico and Tabasco sauce mixture.

6. Chapati Noodles

Ingredients -

3 leftover chapatti

1 tsp Sesame oil

1 tsp Chopped garlic

1 sliced onion

Sliced Carrots

Sliced green pepper

Shredded cabbage

1 tsp Tomato ketchup

1 tsp Red chili sauce

1/2 tsp Soy Sauce

1/2 tsp Lemon juice

1/2 tsp Black pepper

Salt

Direction -

1. Take 3 chapattis and layer it on each other and roll it.

2. Cut chapatti's into very thin strips and separates them.

3. Take a pan preheats on medium heat and adds sesame oil in the pan.

4. Add chopped garlic and sauté it for 30 secs.

5. Add sliced onion and sauté it.

6. Add sliced carrots, green pepper, and shredded cabbage and mix well.

7. Add tomato ketchup, chili sauce, soy sauce, lemon juice, black pepper,

   Salt to taste and mix it well.

8. Add chapatti noodles into the veggies and mix.

9. Garnish it with chopped coriander leaves. And serve hot.

7.Maggi Pakoda

Ingredients –

Maggi noodles 1pkt with tastemaker

Chopped carrot

Chopped capsicum

Chopped cabbage

Chickpea flour

Rice flour 1tbsp

Direction –

1. Firstly boil the water, break the noodles and add the boiling water.
2. Mix it and cook for 5-7 min.
3. Add Maggi tastemaker and mix well.
4. Now turn off the flame.
5. Take it into the separate plate and let it cool down.
6. Then once it cools down, add into the big bowl.
7. And add all veggies.
8. Now add chickpea flour little by little, don't add too much.
9. Add 1tsp of rice flour.
10. Mix it together well.
11. Add a pinch of salt or little salt, since Maggi noodles have some salt in it.

12. Add some hot oil into the mixture, mix it.

13. Take a pan and heat oil, then gently drop into the oil.

14. Fry them; they turn into the golden brown color.

15. When they turn golden brown, take them into the separate plate.

16. In the same way, prepare all the pakodas.

17. I baked some pakoda –spray some oil on the baking tray and place some

Pakoda on the tray.

18. Place the tray in preheated oven till pakodas turn into golden brown color.

19. Once in turn into golden brown, take them out.

20. Turn them into another side; put it again both sides turn into brown take them out.

21. Now the Maggi pakoda and baked Maggi pakoda is ready.

8. Cheesy Maggi Noodles Bread Pockets

Ingredients –

Maggi noodles

5 bread slices

Cheese 1 cup

Maida paste (water + maida, all-purpose flour)

Direction –

1. Take a pan and boil the water.
2. Add in once water comes to boil, add carrots and green peas, boiling it.
3. Then add Maggi noodles (break noodles into small pieces).
4. Once noodles cooked well, add Maggi masala.
5. Mix it well, and cook it for 1 min.
6. Turn off the flame.
7. Trim the edge of bread slices and roll the bread as thin bread.
8. After rolling the bread, its look like a sheet.
9. Repeat the same for all bread slices.
10. Place the stuffing in the middle of the bread and put the cheese also.
11. Apply the maida paste, around the edges.
12. Then fold it and press the edges.
13. Repeat the process cut the uneven edges.

14. Take a pan and heat the oil, and deep fry them.

15. Oil should be hot; otherwise, it will absorb more oil.

16. Fry them on both sides, till they turn into golden brown color.

17. Take out on tissue paper on a plate.

18. If you don't want to deep fry, you can bake them also.

19. Now crispy bread pockets are ready.

20. Serve hot with ketchup.

9. Cheesy Maggi Bread Rolls

Ingredients –

For the cheesy Maggi -

½ cup grated processed cheese

1 packet (70 gms) Maggi noodles, broken into pieces

1 packet Maggi noodles masala

¼ cup chopped capsicum

1 tsp dry red chili flakes

Other ingredients -

2 tbsp plain flour (maida)

13 bread slices

Melted butter for greasing

Direction –

1. Boil 1 cup of water in a deep non-stick pan, and bring it to boil, add the capsicum and Maggi noodles masala, and mix well.

2. And cook on a medium flame for 1 minute, stirring occasionally.

3. Add the Maggi noodles, mix well and cook on a medium flame for 4 minutes or till all the water has been evaporated, stirring occasionally.

4. Add some grated cheese and chili flakes, mix well and cook on a medium flame for 1 minute, stirring occasionally.

5. Divide it into 13 equal portions and keep aside.

6. Now next is, Combine the plain flour and 2 tbsp of water in a small bowl, mix well and keep aside.

7. Remove the edges from all the bread slices and roll each slice with help of a rolling pin (belan).

8. Place one portion of the filling on one side of the bread slice and roll it up tightly.

9. Apply some flour paste (plain flour + water mixture) at the edges and press to seal the stuffing.

10. Repeat steps and make 12 more bread rolls.

11. Apple little melted butter evenly over all the bread rolls and bake them in a pre-heated oven at 180°c (360°f) for 15 minutes or till they turn crisp, turning them once after 10 minutes.

12. Now serves Hot.

10. Maggi Noodle Momos Recipe

Ingredients -

For momos:

1 cup maida / all-purpose flour / plain flour

Salt to taste

2 tsp oil

Water as required to knead the dough

1 tbsp maida / all-purpose flour / plain flour for dusting

Cabbage leaf for placing in the tray

For stuffing:

2 tsp oil

2 cloves garlic (lasun), finely chopped

½ medium sized onion, finely chopped

1 cup carrot, finely chopped

¼ cup cabbage, shreadded

1½ cup water

1 packet maggi masala

1 packet maggi noodles

½ tbsp soy sauce/soya sauce

1 tbsp vinegar

1 tbsp chilli sauce

Direction -

1. Momos dough recipe - firstly, in a large mixing bowl, take 1 cup of maida, salt and oil. mix well.

2. Further add water little by little and knead the dough.

3. Cover and rest for 1 hour.

4. Maggi momos stuffing recipe -firstly, in a large pan heat oil. Sauté garlic and vegetables.

5. Furthermore, add water and get to a boil.

6. Now add Maggi masala and noodles.

7. Mix well and cook till the water is absorbed completely.

8. Now add vinegar, soy sauce, and chilli sauce.

9. Momos preparation recipe: - after an hour pinch a small ball and flatten.

10. Also, dust with some maida and start to roll using a rolling pin.

11. Now place the prepared stuffing in the center.

12. Fold in half forming a semi-circle.

13. Press the edges gently.

14. Further, bring together the tip of folded semi-circles and join them.

15. Furthermore, steam momos for 12 minutes.

16. Finally, serve momos hot with momos sauce and chutney.

11. Vegetable Hakka Noodles

Ingredients:-

150 gms cabbage cut thin lengthwise

150 gms red cabbage cut thin lengthwise

100 gms carrot julliennes

1 no. Green capsicum

50 gms bean sprouts

½ tsp crushed black pepper

1 tbsp dark soy sauce

1 tbsp garlic chopped

1 tbsp chili sauce

1 tbsp oil

1 tsp sesame oil

1 tsp sesame seeds

2-3 stalks springs onion

Salt as required

Direction –

1. Cut the vegetables in juliennes.
2. Heat water in a saucepan and add salt to it.
3. Once the water comes to a boil add the raw noodles and let them cook for 6-7 minutes.
4. Strain the noodles and pour some vegetable oil on them.

5. Take a pan and add some vegetable oil to it and heat till it starts smoking.

6. Now add chopped garlic and fry till golden brown.

7. Then add cabbage, carrots, and capsicum tossing it frequently in the pan on a high flame.

8. Add salt, soy sauce, vinegar, crushed black pepper, chili sauce and give it a quick toss.

9. Now add in the boiled noodles and bean sprouts and mix it well.

10. Finally, add the spring onions and top it all off with sesame oil.

12. Noodles Spring Rolls

Ingredients -

For wrappers -

1 cup of flour

Salt to taste

2 tsp of oil

For Stuffing -

1 cup of noodle

1/4 cup Panner cut into small cubes

½ cup of Cabbage (finely chopped)

¼ cup of Peas

¼ cup of Capsicum (finely chopped)

2 tsp Coriander chopped

1 green Chilli chopped

Half inch Ginger piece finely chopped

1 tsp lemon juice or 1 tsp vinegar

1 tsp soya sauce

¼ tsp black pepper

And salt to taste

Direction -

Method for Wrapper-

1. Knead the flour for making Spring Rolls with Salt and 1 tsp oil. Use lukewarm water for flour.

2. Cover and Leave dough for 10-15 minutes.

Method for Stuffing-

1. Heat a pan with 1 tbsp.

2. Add Ginger finely chopped, sauté it well.

3. Add Green chilli.

4. Add peas and sauté for 2 minutes.

5. Add Capsicum and Cabbage, sauté again for 1.5 minutes.

6. Add paneer cubes.

7. Add salt as per taste and pepper powder.

8. Then add noodles.

9. Soy sauce and lemon juice.

10. Mix all the ingredients well.

11. Stuffing is ready.

12. Now Make 14 small balls of dough, make 2 thin rolls of it off around 6 to 7 inches.

13. Put one roll over other, paste oil in between.

14. Lightly Bake rolls over tava and make 7 rolls.

15. Now separate rolls which we have put over other.

16. Now the roll is thin, fill stuffing and roll all of 14 rolls.

17. Make thin slurry by taking 2 tsp flour and water to stick the rolls.

18. Prepare rest 14 rolls like this.

19. We can shallow fry or deep fry.

20. Fry rolls in minimum flame till it gets golden brown.

21. Now our crispy and tempting spring rolls are ready.

13. Pad Thai Noodles

Ingredients:

1 1/2 cups boiled flat rice noodles

4 tbsp oil

1/2 tbsp chopped garlic

1 cup bean sprouts

3 tbsp roughly chopped roasted peanuts

3/4 cup paneer (cottage cheese) cubes

1 tbsp soy sauce

1 tbsp sugar

1 1/2 tsp chili powder

1 tbsp lemon juice

Salt to taste

1/4 cup chopped spring onion greens

For Garnish

2 tbsp chopped roasted peanuts

1 tbsp chopped spring onion greens

1 tbsp chopped coriander (dhania)

Direction:

1. Heat the oil in a wok/kadhai adds the garlic and sauté for a few seconds.

2. Add the beans sprouts, noodles and peanuts, mix well and cook on a high flame for 2 to 3 minutes, while stirring continuously.

3. Add the paneer, soya sauce, sugar, chili powder, lemon juice, salt, and spring onion greens and cook on a high flame for 2 to 3 minutes, while stirring continuously.

4. Serve hot garnished with peanuts, spring onion greens, and coriander. ENJOY!

14. Chili Garlic Noodles

Ingredient:

Noodles 100 g.

Oil 1 tbsp

Green Chili 4 Number

Garlic (chopped) 4 Number

MSG 1 pinch

Soya sauce 1 tsp

Chili sauce 1 tsp

Butter 1/2 tsp

Spring onions

Directions:

1. Heat oil in a pan add garlic, green Chili, slices of onions, bell pepper, salt, pepper powder, MSG, soy sauce, chili sauce, sauté it.
2. And add pre-boiled noodles toss it and
3. Add butter and spring onions mix it well, switch off the flame.

   ENJOY!

15. Chicken Stir-Fry Noodles

Ingredients:

1 medium carrot (90g), cut into thin strips

1 red pepper (120g), cut into thin strips

1 1/2 inch (4cm) fresh ginger (25g), finely chopped

2 garlic cloves, finely chopped

2 medium green onions, chopped

1 head Broccoli (250g), cut into small florets

7 oz (200g) chicken breast, cut into thin strips

8 oz (230g) dried egg noodles

2 tbsp (24g) sesame oil

1 tsp (5g) brown sugar

3 tbsp (45g) light soy sauce

2 tbsp (30g) Fish/Oyster sauce

Direction:

1. Cook noodles in boiling salted water according to packet instructions. Drain and rinse under cold water. Toss with a little vegetable oil. Set aside until ready to use.

2. Heat oil in a large wok over medium-high heat.

3. Add chicken and toss over high heat until golden. Add garlic and ginger and fry for 30 seconds.

4. Add the vegetables and stir-fry for two-three minutes more over medium-high heat, stirring continuously for even cooking.

5. Add sugar, cooked noodles, soy sauce, and oyster sauce and stir to combine.

6. Serve immediately

16. Bread Rolls With Noodles Stuffing

Ingredients:

Bread - 12

Noodles - 100 grams (boiled)

Green peas - ½ cup

Green coriander - 2 to 3 tbsp (finely chopped)

Lemon - 1

Ginger - 1-inch piece (finely chopped)

Soya sauce - 1 tsp

Salt - ½ tsp or as per taste

Red chili powder - ¼ tsp

Oil - for preparing to stuff or for frying

Direction:

1. Cut off the edges of all the bread slices.
2. Boil noodles till it becomes tender. Strain it and drizzle some oil over it.
3. Take water in a tray to dip bread.
4. Squeeze ½ lemon in a bowl.
5. Heat 1 tsp oil in a pan and add ginger, green chili, and peas into it. Cover and let the peas cook for 1 minute on low flame until tender.
6. Now add salt, red chili powder, green coriander, and lemon juice and soy sauce to the pan. Sauté for a while.

7. Add boiled noodles into the masala. Keep the flame low. Stir all the ingredients well and transfer the stuffing to a plate.

8. Dip the bread slice in water and place it on palm to drain out the excess water completely.

9. Place 1-1.5 tsp stuffing over the bread slices and rolls nicely to close the stuffing. Similarly, prepare all the bread rolls.

10. Heat enough oil in a pan for deep frying the bread rolls. Gently slide 2-3 bread rolls to the oil and deep fry until crispy and golden brown.

11. Drain out the fried bread rolls over kitchen paper towels to remove excess oil. Bread rolls are ready to serve.

12. Serve this lip smacking and crunchy noodles stuffed bread rolls with a side accompaniment of any Indian dip or chutney like coriander chutney, mint chutney, tomato ketchup and relish eating.

Suggestions

1. Immediately take the bread slice out while dipping it in the water and squeeze it. Otherwise, it will become too soft and cannot be rolled.

2. Make sure that the stuffing in the covered with bread really well. Else oil will enter the rolls while frying them.

17.Shrimp And Vegetable Stir Fry Noodles

Ingredients:

14 oz already cooked or dry noodles (cook dry noodles according to package instruction)

1 pound Shrimp

1 Tbs. Sesame oil

1 medium onion

2 cloves garlic

1 tsp chopped ginger

3/4 cup sliced carrots (use more if you want)

3/4 cup broccoli (use more if you want)

1 Tablespoon oyster sauce

1Tablespoon soy sauce

1 teaspoon brown sugar

1/2 cup chopped spring onions

Salt and pepper to taste

Direction:

1. Heat oil in a pan add shrimp stir
2. Add some salt and pepper cook for abour2-5 minutes
3. Don't overcook the shrimp switch off flame
4. Take out shrimp in a bowl and set aside
5. Now again in the same pan add sesame oil

6. After heating oil add in chopped onions

7. Fry the onions on medium heat till it becomes translucent

8. Add in some chopped garlic and ginger fry till it fragrant don't burn the garlic

9. Add in some carrot, broccoli, salt, and pepper mix everything together

10. And cook for about 4-5 minutes on high heat

11. Add in already cooked noodles toss it

12. Add in oyster sauce, soy sauce, brown sugar, and cooked shrimp

13. Mix everything well and cook for about 3 minutes on high heat

14. Add in chopped spring onion cook again for about 3 minutes on high heat

15. The Delicious dish is ready. ENJOY!

18. Left-Over Roti Noodles

Ingredients:

2 leftover roti

2 tbsp. sliced tomatoes

2 tbsp. sliced capsicum

2 tbsp. sliced onion

2 tbsp. chopped carrots

1 finely sliced green chili

Salt to taste

¼ tsp. red chili powder

¼ tsp. pav bhaji masala

Pinch of black pepper

Tomato ketchup as required (optional)

1 ½ tsp. oil

¼ tsp. cumin seed

¼ tsp. finely chopped garlic

¼ tsp. grated ginger

Freshly chopped coriander leaves

Direction:

1. Cut each roti in long strips and 1/4 inch thick
2. Heat oil in a pan
3. Once the oil became hot add cumin seed and cook till it becomes light brown
4. Add sliced onion, garlic and ginger

5. Sauté it on medium heat till onion becomes light brown

6. Add in sliced tomato, chili, capsicum, and carrots cook on medium heat for 2 minutes

7. Add salt in it sauté it on medium heat for 3-4 minutes or till it becomes little soft

8. Add all the spices mix it well

9. Now add roti pieces and black pepper powder

10. Add tomato ketchup as per taste

11. Garnish with coriander leaves and serve!

19. Singapore Noodles

Ingredients

160 g rice noodles

2 Goat steaks

1 tbsp honey

1 tbsp soy sauce

2 tsp corn flour

1 red onion

10 g ginger

2 cloves garlic

1 red chili

100 g shiitake mushrooms

1/4 Savoy cabbage

2 tbsp vegetable oil

1 tbsp curry powder

1 tsp Chinese 5 spice

1 tbsp rice wine vinegar

1 tbsp sesame oil

150 g raw king prawns

100 g water chestnuts

1 lime

2 spring onions

Direction:

1. Soak the noodles in cold water

2. MARINATE THE Goat Meat

3. Slice the Goat Meat steaks as thinly as possible then toss with honey, 1 tbsp soy sauce and the corn flour.

4. Peel and slice the onion slice the mushrooms and cabbage leaves. Peel and mince the ginger, garlic, and chili. Set all aside for later.

5. Grab a wok or pan over a high heat until smoking hot then add the veg. oil and Goat Meat to fry for a couple of minutes keeping it moving on the pan occasionally, then scoop out and back into the bowl.

6. Tip the prepared vegetables (except for the cabbage) into the wok and fry everything for another few minutes. Add the spices, sesame oil, rice wine vinegar, the king prawns and the sliced cabbage.

7. Fry until the prawns are completely pink and cooked through. Add the soaked and drained noodles and the water chestnuts then toss everything together until the noodles are piping hot, then add the Goat back in.

8. Squeeze over the lime juice and serve everything in a big bowl.

9. Scatter over the spring onions and drizzle with a little extra sesame oil.

20. Singapore Rice Noodle

Ingredients:

Shrimp

Chicken

Egg

Rice noodle

Green and Red Bell Peppers

Onions

Bean Sprout

Curry powder

Oysters sauce

Light soy sauce

Dark Soya Sauce

Direction:

1. Heat oil in a wok or deep pan break the egg into it scramble
2. Then add chopped pepper and onion in it stir and fry
3. Add shrimp, chicken and bean sprout cook them well
4. Add boiled noodles and all the spices and all three sauces
5. Mix and toss for 2 minutes

6. Singapore rice noodles are ready. ENJOY!

21. Hong Kong Style Wonton Noodle Soup

Ingredients:

Hong Kong Style Egg Noodles

Wonton Skin

Goat Meat

Shrimp

Chicken Stock

White pepper

Sugar

Salt

Soy sauce

Sesame Oil

Direction:

1. Add Goat Meat, onion, one egg, 1 tsp. salt, 1 tsp. sugar in a grinder
2. Sprinkle some white pepper and grind them together
3. Now take a slice of wonton skin apply egg thin layer on it
4. Then put 1 tsp. of mixture we prepare earlier
5. And cover it properly by skin and make a roll
6. Prepare all roll same like this
7. Boil some noodles take aside
8. Now boil these rolls too until they come on top

9. Now take them out

10. Now add sesame oil sugar salt soya sauce and chicken stock in a deep vessel

11. Put it on flame stir

12. Now take noodles in a dish put boiled rolls on it

13. Garnish with spring onion and now fill in this the stock mixture

14. Delicious soup is ready

22. Classic Singapore Noodles

Ingredients:

1 egg

125g rice vermicelli, soaked 1/2 hr in hot water, drained and rinsed with cold water.

1/2 onion, sliced

1/4 red bell pepper, diced

2 small scallions, chopped

Few prawns

1-inch piece Chinese bbq Goat Meat, sliced into strips

1 handful bean sprouts

2 teaspoons curry powder

3 tablespoons oil

1 tablespoon oyster sauce

1 tablespoon light soy sauce

1 teaspoon salt

few drops sesame oil

Direction:

1. Heat oil in a pan break egg in it scramble it fry
2. Remove it from pan
3. Now fry sliced onions and prawns
4. Add in diced red pepper, rice, and Goat Meat
5. Add curry powder and stir well
6. Now add fried egg and scallion

7. Add in soy sauce and oyster sauce mix properly
8. Add bean sprouts mix and stir continuously
9. Add little bit if water if noodles get dry
10. Add a few drops of sesame oil
11. Keep stirring to combine mix well
12. Add salt stir well
13. Classic Singapore noodles are ready.

23. Quick Peanut Butter Noodles

Ingredients:

5 tbsp crunchy peanut butter

1 tbsp dark soy sauce

1 tbsp rice wine vinegar

3 tbsp chili oil

1 tsp sesame oil

1 clove garlic, finely grated

1 thumb sized piece ginger, finely grated

1 red chili, finely sliced

400g udon noodles

6 spring onions, finely sliced

2 tbsp sesame seeds, toasted

Direction:

1. Cook the noodles in boiling water until tender.

2. While the noodles cook, in a small saucepan over a medium heat whisk together the peanut butter, soy sauce, rice wine vinegar, oils, garlic, and ginger until smooth.

3. Loosen the mixture with a little water, adding a tablespoon at a time until you are left with a sauce. When it comes to a steady simmer, lower the heat and keep it warm.

4. Drain the noodles and while they are still hot, toss through the peanut butter sauce.

5. Add the chili, spring onions and sesame seeds and toss again. Serve straight away

6. Serve straight away

24. Mie Goreng Indonesian Stir-Fried Noodles

Ingredients

For the Sauce

1 tsp soy sauce

1 Tbs. Keycap Manis (Indonesian sweet soy sauce)

1 Tbs. Sambal (chili paste)

1 tsp dark soy sauce

1/4 cup chicken stock

For Stir Fry

6 oz egg noodles- dry, fresh, semi-fresh doesn't matter, just prepare by following the package you are using.

2 Tbs. cooking oil, divided

3 to 4 oz shrimp or any other protein you prefer

2 cloves garlic, chopped (approximately 2 tsp)

1/2 shallot, chopped (approximately 1/4 cup)

1 oz carrot, julienned (approximately 2 Tbs.)

3 oz green leaf vegetable such as Yu Choy, Bok choy, green cabbage and etc

3 oz bean sprouts

1 Tbs. fried shallot

1 egg

Direction:

1. Heat 1 tbsp. oil in a pan add shrimp to the pan

2. Add salt and pepper and fry
3. Once fried Remove shrimp and take aside
4. Heat again 1 tbsp. of oil in a pan add garlic and shallot
5. Once fried add vegetables and fry them
6. Now add noodles and sauce keep stirring for 3-4 minutes to combine them well
7. Add bean sprouts and fried shrimp mix well for 2-3 minutes
8. Garnish with fried shallots remove from heat
9. Finish it by placing the fried egg on top

25. Chinese Hand Pulled Noodles

Ingredients:

1kg plain flour

600ml water

4 tablespoons oil

Direction:

1. Place the flour in a large bowl, and gradually mix in 600ml water. Bring the dough together and knead until smooth, 15 to 20 minutes.

2. Cover with cling film and rest for 15 minutes. Knead again for 2 minutes, then re-cover and let rest for another 15 minutes. Finally, knead the dough one more time for 2 minutes.

3. Divide the dough into 4 equal pieces. Roll each piece to 1cm thick. Brush both sides of each sheet with oil, and then stack them together. Cover with cling film and set aside for 10 to 15 minutes.

4. Fill a large saucepan with water and bring to the boil.

5. Place one of the sheets of dough on a cutting board and slice into 5mm wide strips. Use both hands to hold the two ends of the strip, and pull and stretch to 80 to 90cm long, fold it in thirds and pull again to the same length.

6. Shake and slam it several times, then drop it into the boiling water immediately to cook. The length of one strip of noodle should be around 2 to 3 meters.

Add 2 to 3 more strips of noodles to the boiling water; cook each serving of noodles for a total of 5 to 10 minutes.

7. Repeat the process with the remaining sheets of dough, serving each bowl of noodles as you finish cooking them.

8. Place the drained noodles in a serving bowl and use with your favorite recipe

26. Noodles Samosa

Ingredients:

All-purpose flour- 1 cup

Carom seeds - ¼ tsp

Salt - ¼ tsp (as per taste)

Ghee - 2 tbsp

For stuffing:

Noodles - 1 cup (boiled)

Mushrooms - 2 (finely chopped)

Carrot - ¼ cup (thinly sliced)

Green peas - ¼ tsp

Salt - ¼ tsp

Red chili powder - ¼ tsp

Black pepper powder - ¼ tsp

Green coriander - 2-3 tbsp

Lemon juice - 1 tsp

Soya sauce - ½ tsp

Green chili - 1 (finely chopped)

Ginger - ½ inch piece (grated) (½ tsp paste)

Direction:

1. Firstly knead dough for making samosa. For this take all-purpose flour in a bowl, add ghee, salt and carom seeds. Mix all ingredients really well

2. Add a little water at a time and knead a hard dough.

3. Cover the dough and keep it aside for the ½ hour for fermenting. Meanwhile, prepare to stuff for the samosas.

Stuffing for Chinese samosas:

1. Add 2 tbsp oil in a pan and place it on flame for heating. Add ginger, green chili, green peas and sauté for 2 minutes.

2. Also, add chopped carrots and sauté for 1 minute. Now add mushrooms, salt, red chili powder, black pepper powder, and soy sauce and lemon juice.

3. Cook for 1 minute and add boiled noodles and green coriander leaves. Mix all ingredients nicely. Stuffing is ready

How to make samosa:

1. Knead the dough and make it soft. Divide into four equal parts and make round balls.

2. Take one ball, with help of rolling pin roll the ball in an oval shape thinly.

3. Divide the rolled puri into two equal halves.

4. Take one part and place it on your hand, put some water on the edges with help of finger and paste the second corner giving it a round shape.

5. Now stuff it with filling. Keep ½ inch space empty from the top and put water all around.

6. Give a plate at the back and stick the samosa from the top.

7. Place the ready samosa in any plate. Likewise, make all samosas.

How to fry samosas:

1. Take oil in a pan and place it on flame for heating. When oil gets medium hot, gently place 3-4 or as many samosas as possible in the pan.

2. Fry on the medium or low flame until they turn golden brown in color. Likewise, fry all samosas.

3. Piping hot and crusty noodles samosas are ready. Serve noodles samosas with green coriander chutney, tamarind sweet chutney or tomato sauce.

Suggestion:

For making stuffing you can use any of your favorite vegetables.

For boiling noodles:

1. Take enough water in a pan so that noodles get drenched nicely. When water starts boiling, add 1 tsp oil and noodles.

2. When noodles become tender take them out and drain the excess water. Pour some cold water and wash them.

27. Vegetable And Noodle Soup

Ingredients

1/2 cup shredded cabbage

1/4 cup sliced colored capsicum (red, yellow and green)

1/2 cup bean sprouts

1/4 cup grated carrot

3/4 cup boiled noodles

1 1/2 tbsp oil

salt to taste

a few drops of soy sauce

For Serving

soya sauce

Chilies in vinegar

Chili sauce

Direction:

1. Heat the oil in a wok/ pan, add the cabbage, capsicum, bean sprouts and carrot, mix well and sauté on a high flame for 1 to 2 minutes.

2. Add the noodles, mix well and cook on a high flame for 1 minute.

3. Add 2 cups of hot water, salt and soy sauce, mix well and cook on a medium flame for 2 to 3 minutes, while stirring occasionally.

4. Serve hot with soy sauce, chilies in vinegar, chili sauce.

28. Vegetable Noodles

Ingredients -

8-10 button mushrooms, sliced

1 small carrot, cut into strips

½ cup bean sprouts

1 stalk spring onion greens, finely chopped

3 cups boiled noodles

2 tablespoons oil

1-inch ginger, finely chopped

1 tablespoon chopped garlic

1 tablespoon green chili sauce

1 teaspoon soy sauce

Crushed black peppercorns to taste

Salt to taste

Direction -

1. Take a pan and heat oil.

2. Now add ginger and sauté for 30 seconds.

3. Add garlic and sauté till golden. And add mushrooms and carrot.

4. Toss to mix and cook till mushrooms are done.

5. Add noodles and toss on high heat to mix.

6. Now add green chili sauce and soy sauce and mix well.

7. Add crushed peppercorns and salt and mix well again.

8. Now add bean sprouts and spring onion (greens) and toss to mix well.

9. Serve hot garnished with bell pepper curls.

29. Chicken Hakka Noodles Recipe

INGREDIENTS:-

For Boiling Noodles -

Noodles -1 packet

Oil 1 tbsp

Salt 1 tsp.

Chicken, spices, and veggies -

Boneless Chicken cut in Julienne ½ kg / 500 gm

Spring Onion Whites ½ Cup

Onion Sliced 1 Medium

Capsicum (Julienne) Medium 1

Carrot (Julienne) 1 Medium

Garlic Chopped 2 Tbsp

Ginger Chopped 2 tsp

Spring Onion Greens ½ Cup

Julienne Cabbage ½ Cup

Chopped Green Chilies 2 tsp

Soya Sauce 3 tbsp

Vinegar 2 tbsp

Salt 1 tsp + 1 1/2 tsp Or to taste

Black pepper 1 tsp + 1 tsp

Red Chili Flakes 1 ½ tsp

Oil ½ to ¾ Cup

Direction –

1. Boil the noodles with 1 tbsp of oil & 1.5 tsp of salt till it done. It shouldn't be too much soft.

2. Once boiled, rinse the noodles with cold water 1-2 times and set aside.

3. Take a pan and add oil.

4. When heat oil adds Ginger and garlic and sautés well.

5. Before their color changes add chicken with 1 tsp of salt & black pepper and add 1 tbsp of Vinegar and Soya Sauce.

6. Keep the flame high and stir fry the chicken.

7. When the chicken is the cook, add onions (both, green also) and mix well for 1-2 minutes.

8. Add Carrots and keep mixing

9. Add in Capsicum, Cabbage, Noodles and black pepper powder, soya sauce, add some chili

Sauce, vinegar, and green onion.

10. Keep Tossing on high flame. Engaged both hands using spatulas while tossing.

11. Last, add Spring Onions Greens on top and give the last mix.

12. Adjust salt and spices according to your taste and serve.

30. Chicken Chow Mein Recipe

Ingredients:-

Chow mein sauce –

Oyster sauce 1 tbsp

Soy sauce 2 tbs

Sesame oil 1 tsp

(Sugar) 1 tbs (optional)

Kali Mirch Powder (Black pepper powder) 1 tsp

(White pepper powder) ½ tsp

Corn flour 2 tbsp

Chicken boneless cut in strips 250 gms

Chow mein sauce 1 tbs

Oil 2 tbs

(Garlic) finely chopped 1 tbs

(Carrot) julienne ½ Cup

(Cabbage) shredded 2 Cups

Shimla Mirch (Capsicum) julienne ½ Cup

(Green onion white part) julienne ¼ Cup

Sirka (Vinegar) 2 tbs

Chow mein or Egg noodles (Boiled) 1 & ½ Cups

Yakhni (Chicken stock) ¼ Cup

Namak (Salt) ½ tsp or to taste

Hara pyaz (Green onion) julienne ½ Cup

Kali Mirch (Black Pepper) crushed ½ tsp

Direction –

1. Take a bowl, add oyster sauce, soy sauce, sesame oil, sugar, black pepper powder, white pepper powder, corn flour and mix well. This is a Chow Mein sauce is ready.

2. Now in chicken, add 1 tbs of chow mein sauce, mix well and marinate for 15 minutes.

3. Take a pan, add oil, garlic and marinated chicken, stir-fry until chicken changes color.

4. Add carrot and mix, add cabbage, capsicum, green onion white part and stir-fry for 1-2 minutes.

5. Add remaining chow mein sauce, vinegar and mix well.

6. Add chow mein or egg noodles, chicken stock, salt, green onion and stir-fry for 2-3 minutes on high flame.

7. And last Sprinkle black pepper crushed and serves.

31. Japchae (Glass Noodles Stir-Fried With Vegetables)

Ingredients –

4 ounces beef, filet mignon (or Goat shoulder), cut into ¼ inch wide and 2½ inch long strips

2 large dried shitake mushroom soaked in warm water for 2 to 3 hours, cut into thin strips

2 garlic cloves, minced

1 tablespoons plus 2 teaspoons sugar

2 tablespoons plus 1 teaspoon soy sauce

2 tablespoons sesame oil

1 tablespoon toasted sesame seed

1 large egg

4 ounces spinach, washed and drained

4 ounces of dungeon (sweet potato starch noodles)

2 to 3 green onions, cut crosswise into 2 inch long pieces

1 medium onion (1 cup), sliced thinly

4 to 5 white mushrooms, sliced thinly

1 medium carrot (¾ cup), cut into matchsticks

½ red bell pepper, cut into thin strips (optional)

ground black pepper

salt

vegetable oil

Direction -

1. Marinate the beef and mushrooms-Put the beef and shiitake mushrooms into a bowl and mix with 1 clove of minced garlic, 1 teaspoon sugar, ¼ teaspoon ground black pepper, 2 teaspoons soy sauce, and 1 teaspoon of sesame oil with a wooden spoon or by hand. Cover and keep it in the fridge.

2. Make the egg garnish (jidan) - Crack the egg and separate the egg yolk from the egg white.

3. Remove the white stringy stuff (chalaza) from the yolk. Beat with a pinch of salt with a fork.

4. Add 1 teaspoon of vegetable oil to a heat nonstick pan.

5. Swirl the oil around so it covers the pan, and then wipe off the excess heated oil with a kitchen towel or any clean cloth so only a thin layer remains on the pan.

6. To keep the jidan as yellow as possible, turn off the heat and pour the egg yolk mixture into the pan.

7. Now till it around so the mixture spreads thinly.

8. Let it cook using the remaining heat in the pan for about 1 minute. Flip it over and let it the pan for 1 more minute.

9. Let it cool and slice it into thin strips.

10. Prepare the noodles and vegetables - Bring a large pot or deep pan of water to a boil.

11. Add the spinach and blanch for 30 seconds to 1 minute, then take it out with a slotted spoon or strainer.

12. Let the water keep boiling to cook the noodles.

13. Rinse the spinach in cold water to stop it from cooking.

14. Squeeze it with your hands to remove any excess water. Cut it a few times and put it into a bowl.

15. Add in 1 teaspoon soy sauce and 1 teaspoon sesame oil and mix it.

16. Put it into a large mixing bowl.

17. Put the noodles into the boiling water, cover and cook for 1 minute.

18. Stir them with a wooden spoon so they don't stick together.

19. Cover and keep cooking for another 7 minutes until the noodles are soft.

20. Strain and cut them a few times with kitchen scissors.

21. Put the noodles into the large bowl next to the spinach.

22. Add 2 teaspoons sesame oil, 1 teaspoon soy sauce, and 1 teaspoon sugar. Mix well by hand or a wooden spoon.

23. This process will season the noodles and also keep the noodles from sticking to each other.

24. Heat a pan over medium-high heat. Add 2 teaspoons vegetable oil with the onion, the green onion, and a pinch of salt. Stir-fry about 2 minutes until the onion looks a little translucent.

25. And Transfer to the noodle bowl.

26. Heat up the pan again and add 2 teaspoons vegetable oil. Add the white mushrooms and a pinch of salt.

27. Stir-fry for 2 minutes until softened and a little juicy. Transfer to the noodle bowl.

28. Heat up the pan and add 1 teaspoon vegetable oil.

29. Add the carrot and stir-fry for 20 seconds. Add the red bell pepper strips and stir-fry another 20 seconds.

30. And Transfer to the noodle bowl.

31. Heat up the pan again and add 2 teaspoons vegetable oil. Add the beef and mushroom mixture.

32. And stir fry for a few minutes until the beef is no longer pink and the mushrooms are softened and shiny.

33. Transfer to the noodle bowl.

34. Add 1 minced garlic clove, 1 tablespoon soy sauce, 1 tablespoon sugar, ½ teaspoon ground black pepper, and 2 teaspoons of sesame oil to the mixing bowl full of ingredients. Mix all together by hand.

35. Add the egg garnish and 1 tablespoon sesame seeds. Mix it.

36. And serve it to a large plate and Enjoy.

32. Maggi/Ramen Masala Recipe

Ingredients –

Maggi noodles-2 packet (you may use any noodles like yippee or top ramen)

Green chili (chopped)-1

Curry leaves-8 to 10

Green peas (fresh/frozen)-25 gm

Tomato (chopped)-1

Onion (chopped)-1 large

Cooking oil- 3 tbsp

Turmeric powder-1/4 tsp

Red chili powder-1/3 tsp

Cumin powder- 1/4 tsp

Coriander powder-1/4 tsp

Salt-1/4 tsp

Direction -

1. Take a pan and heat oil.

2. Now heat the oil add in chopped onion, add green chili and curry leaves and sauté well 2min. on medium flame.

3. Add in green peas (frozen) sauté well cook 1mins.

4. Add in chopped tomato and sauté for 2-3 min on a low-med flame.

5. Now cooked all ingredients then the flame is low.

6. Now add turmeric powder, add red chili powder, cumin powder, coriander powder and last add salt to taste.

7. Now mix well and cook for ½min.

8. Add maggi tastemaker, and mix well.

9. Add 2 cup water increase the flame and mix well.

10. Now cover it and boil 1 min.

11. Open the lid and stir it and add noodles.

12. And mix it well till noodles are soft.

13. Reduce the flame is low, cook it for 1 min on medium flame without cover.

14. Stir it after 1min.

15. Now cover it and cook for ½ min on medium flame.

16. Open the lid and stir it.

17. Now take out in the serving bowl.

33. Maggi Noodles Spring Roll

Ingredients -

1/4 cup shredded cabbage

1/2 capsicum cut lengthwise

1 spring onion cut lengthwise

4-5 French beans cross cut

Maggi noodles and taste maker

1 cup of tomato sauce

1 tablespoon oil

1/2 teaspoon ginger chili paste

1 teaspoon chat masala

Salt to taste

Tabasco or capsico sauce

Plain flour paste

Direction -

To make the filling -

1. Take a pan and heat 1 tbsp. oil. add capsicum and french beans and sauté for 2 minutes.

2. Add Maggi noodles.

3. Add water and let the mixture boil. Add the tastemaker.

4. Add ginger chili paste, add chat masala, add 1 and 1/2 tbsp. tomato ketchup, shredded cabbage, and spring onions Add salt as per taste and mix well.

5. Add salt as per taste and mix well.

To make the rolls -

1. Take one spring roll sheet.
2. Spread the noodles mixture over the sheets.
3. Make tight rolls covering up the noodle mixture completely.
4. Fix the edges of the rolls with plain flour paste and deep fry the rolls.
5. Cut the rolls in pieces once they cool down a bit.
6. Serve with capsico and Tabasco sauce mixture.

34. Noodles Tava Cutlet

Ingredients:

Noodles 1 cup Salt to taste

Onion 1 small cup

Carrot 1 small cup

Coriander leaves 1 bunch

Green chilies 2-3 no's

Pepper powder 1 pinch

Spinach 1 small cup

Coriander powder ½ tsp

Lime juice 2-3 tsp

Oats powder 1 small cup

All-purpose flour 3 tsp

Breadcrumb 1 cup

Oil 2 tsp

Direction –

1. Boil the noodles till soft or mushy consistency with salt in it.

2. Add finely chopped onions, chopped carrots, green chilies, finely chopped coriander leaves, pepper powder, spinach, coriander powder, lime juice (also add chat masala/amchur powder), salt and mix it well carefully.

3. Now add oats powder (optional add any other flour) and mix it again.

4. Make dumplings with your hands and keep it aside.

5. If it's sticking to your hands apply some water to your hands.

6. Make small tikkis with the dumplings.

7. And make the slurry of all-purpose flour, salt, and water.

8. Dip these tikkis in the slurry both the sides and coat them with bread crumb.

9. Take a Pan or tawa and heat fries them some oil.

10. Place all the tikki's on the pan and cook on medium flame.

11. Cook both the sides till they turn golden brown.

12. Take them on a plate and serve with tomato ketchup.

35. Triple Schezwan Noodles

Ingredients:

Noodles dried - 200 grams

Oil (for noodles) - 1 table spoon

Salt - To taste

Oil - to deep fry

Other Ingredients

Carrot - 1 medium sized

French beans - 4 to 6

Spring onions - 2

Ginger chopped - 1-inch piece

Garlic chopped - 4 to 6 cloves

Sichuan peppercorns - 8 to 10

Chilli flakes - 1 tablespoon

Peppercorns - 8 to 10

Red Chili Paste - 1 tablespoon

Ajinomoto - 1/4 teaspoon

Bean Sprouts - 1/2 cup

White Pepper Powder - 1/4 teaspoon

Vinegar - 1 tablespoon

Oil - 2 tablespoon

Salt - To taste

For garnishing

Fine chopped Green Spring onion

Direction –

1. First, boil the noodles in water add in water some salt.
2. After Cook, the noodles drain water.
3. And now fries the noodles in deep oil.
4. Then some noodles are fried for the last topping.
5. Take a pan and heat oil.
6. Add in chopped fresh beans, add chopped spring onion, chopped garlic, and add

Grated carrot and sauté well.

7. Shezwan – some crushed black pepper, some crushed Sichuan peppercorns - 8 to 10, add 1 tsp red chili flakes.
8. Now add noodles to the pan and toss it well.
9. Now a small bowl adds red chili paste, add some water and mix well (diluted).
10. Red chili pastes and adds on noodles.
11. Add on crushed ingredients on noodles.
12. And now mix well toss well on high flame.
13. Add beans sprout (Ankur whole mung), mix well.
14. Add chopped green onion, add some white pepper powder.
15. Mix well it and last add the vinegar.
16. Now add crushed fry noodles and mix it.
17. Now serves hot on the plate and garnish some fry noodles.

36. Shanghai Stewed Noodles

Ingredients:

Chopped Cabbage ¼ (cut into 1-inch pieces)

Sliced button Mushroom 2

Spring onion 1

Noodles 200 gm.

Oil 1 tbsp.

Sliced Onion medium 1

Crushed garlic 6-8 cloves

Sliced half carrot

Capsicum 1 (cut into 1-inch pieces)

Salt

White pepper powder ½ tsp.

Direction:

1. Heat oil in a pan adds sliced onion and crushed garlic
2. Mix and stir well on high heat
3. Add in spring onion, mushroom sauté it
4. Add carrot, capsicum, and salt
5. Add in white pepper powder mix properly
6. Add noodle in it mix
7. Add vegetable stock and corn flour in it mix well
8. Cook until soup gets thick
9. Serve it hot!

37. Thukpa - Tibetan Noodle Soup

Ingredients:

For the Soup:

Oil - 1 tbsp

Garlic - 1 tbsp, minced

Green Chili - to taste

Onion - 1 small, chopped

Tomato - 1 medium, chopped

Cabbage - 1 cup, chopped

Salt - to taste

Red Chili Powder - to taste

Garam Masala - 1 tsp

Chicken Masala - 1/2 tsp (optional)

Water - 3 cups

Vegetable Cubes - 1 or as needed

Cilantro - 5 sprigs, chopped

For the Noodles:

Tibetan Noodles or any noodles of your choice - 5oz (approx. 150gm)

Water - 3 cups

Oil - 1 tsp

Salt - 1/2 tsp

For the Omelet:

Eggs - 2

Oil - 1 tsp

Salt - a pinch

Direction:

For the Soup:

1. In a pressure cooker, heat Oil on medium heat.
2. Add Garlic and Green Chilies. Cook for 30 seconds.
3. Add in Onions and cook until translucent. Mix frequently.
4. Add in Tomatoes and Cabbage. Mix and cook till the vegetables get soft.
5. Add in the dry spices - Salt, Red Chili Powder, and Garam Masala. Mix and cook for 30 seconds.
6. If you have Chicken Masala, add along with the dry spices.
7. Add Vegetable Cube and Water and allow the cube to dissolve.
8. Close Pressure Cooker and cook 2 whistles.
9. Allow the pressure to release.
10. Once safe, open and add chopped Cilantro. Adjust spices as needed.

For the Noodles:

11. Boil Water and add Salt.

12. Add in the Noodles and cook as per package directions.
13. Once done, drain all the Water and mix in the Oil.

For the Omelet:
14. Crack the egg into a bowl and beat it well.
15. Add a pinch of Salt.
16. Heat Oil on medium heat in a small skillet.
17. Pour the Egg mixture spread and allow it to cook on the bottom side.
18. Flip and cook on the other side as well.
19. Remove and cut strips and keep aside.

For Assembly:
20. In a deep bowl, add in half the cooked Noodles.
21. Pour in half the Soup.
22. Add in the Omelet strips.
23. Garnish with Cilantro.
24. Enjoy.

Tips:
25. Add in vegetables of your choice example: Carrots, Spinach, and Mushrooms.
26. Use Vegetable broth instead of the Vegetable cube and water in the Soup.
27. Want to make a Chicken Version:

a. Wash 2-3 pieces of Chicken with bones.

b. Boil the Chicken with 3 cups of Water.

c. Add a bit of Salt, a Bay Leaf, Cinnamon Stick, 2 Cloves, Quarter Onion, 2 cloves of Garlic, and a small pcs. Of Ginger.

d. Allow it to boil well.

e. Once the Chicken is cooked, remove and allow it to cool down and shred or cut into pieces.

f. Boil the balance of the Water for another 10-15 min.

g. Strain and use the liquid instead of the water and the Vegetable Cube, in the recipe for the Soup mentioned above.

h. Add in the shredded Chicken right before serving.

i. You can add half the amount of Vegetables mentioned above if makes the Non-Vegetarian version

38. Korean Ramyeon

Ingredients:

1 package of Korean ramyeon

2½ cups water

1 egg

2 green onions, chopped

Directions:

1. Bring the water to a boil over high heat.
2. Add the noodles and the included soup powder to the boiling water. Cover and boil for 1 minute.
3. Open the lid and turn the ramyeon over with a spoon.
4. Crack the egg directly into the boiling ramyeon, and cover and cook for 1 to 2 minutes. Don't stir, so the egg will be poached.
5. Remove from the heat. Open the lid and add the green onions and the included package of dried vegetables. Serve with kimchi and rice.

39. Korean Noodle Soup

Ingredients:

10 ounces somyeon (thin wheat flour noodles)

1 tablespoon toasted sesame seeds, ground

Semi circles sheet of gim (seaweed paper), toasted, crushed in a plastic bag to make seaweed flakes

2 poached eggs (optional)

For the anchovy stock (makes 10 cups' worth):

14 cups of water

8 ounces Korean radish or daikon, sliced thinly

4 green onion roots

2 medium size onions (12 ounces), sliced

20 large dried anchovies, heads and guts are removed

1 ounce dried kelp

2½ teaspoons salt

For the spicy kimchi mix:

4 green onions, chopped

4 ounces of chopped fermented kimchi (about ½ to 2/3 cup)

2 tablespoons hot pepper paste

Shaoxing teaspoon honey

2 teaspoons sesame oil

Directions:

Make the stock:

1. Combine the water, radish, and onion, green onion roots, anchovies, and kelp in a large saucepan, cover, and cook over medium-high heat for 30 minutes.

2. Turn down the heat to low and boil another 20 minutes.

3. Turn off the heat and strain. You will get about 10 cups of stock. Stir in the salt.

4. Make the spicy kimchi mix:

5. Add all ingredients to a bowl and mix well. Set aside

Cook the noodles:

6. Bring 10 cups of water to a boil. Add the noodles and stir them with a wooden spoon so that they don't stick together.

7. Cover and cook over medium heat for 3-4 minutes until they start boiling over.

8. Open, lower the heat to low, and stir. Cook another minute until the noodles is nicely cooked.

9. Take a sample: it should be chewy but there shouldn't be anything hard in it as you chew.

10. Strain and rinse the noodles in cold water a couple of times. Strain them.

11. Divide the noodles into 2 portions and put each portion into a serving bowl or pot.

Make guksu:

12. Use a strainer and a ladle to put a bit of bubbling hot stock over the noodles, and then drain it back out into the stockpot so it can be heated again.

13. Do this a couple of times until the noodles are heated up.

14. Add 2 or 2½ cups of the hot stock to the noodles. Place the kimchi mixture, ground sesame seeds, and gimgaru (crushed seaweed flakes) in the center of the noodle soup

15. Add a poached egg on top if you made one.

16. Serve hot and eat immediately.

40. Quick Ramen Noodle Soup

Ingredients:

1 tbsp grape seed oil

1 tbsp minced garlic

1/2 tsp grated ginger

4 scallions, sliced (white and green parts)

1/2 tsp chili sauce

3 cups chicken stock

3 cups beef broth

1 tbsp fish sauce

1 tbsp soy sauce

1 cup water

4 eggs, optional

1 lb lo mien, ramen, or so men noodles

Directions:

1. Place the grape seed oil, garlic, ginger, scallions, and chili sauce in a Dutch oven or large pot and cook over medium-high heat for 2-3 minutes, until fragrant and the scallions start to soften.

2. Add the chicken stock, beef stock, fish sauce, and soy sauce and bring to a boil over high heat.

3. Taste and adjust as necessary (I add about a cup of water to reduce saltiness).

4. Add your eggs, if cooking and the noodles to the boiling soup, and cook for about 3 minutes (the noodles I use require about 3 minutes, but follow the package instructions).

5. Serve and enjoy!

41.Schezwan Paneer Noodles

Ingredients:

Noodles 1 packet

Onion 2

Capsicum 1

Carrot 1

Garlic

Cabbage 1

Slit Green chili 4-5

Spring onion 2tsp.

Cottage cheese cube ½ cup

Soy sauce 2 tsp.

Chili sauce 1tsp.

Schezwan sauce 2 tsp.

Black pepper powder 1 tsp.

Salt to taste

Oil ½ cup

Direction:

1. Boiled noodles in a pan by adding 3 cups of water, salt, and 2 tsp. oil
2. After boiling wash the noodles in cold water and set aside
3. Now heat a pan add 3 tbs. oil
4. Once the oil heated add onion, capsicum, garlic, carrot and green chili stir well for 2 minutes
5. Add in spring onion, cabbage, salt and cheese cube stir and cook on low heat
6. Add all three sauce mix well
7. Add black pepper powder stir and cook for 2 minutes
8. Now add cooked noodles in it mix together
9. Delicious noodles are ready. Serve hot!

42. Paneer Noodles

Ingredients:

2-3 nest of Noodles

200 grams Paneer (Cut lengthwise)

2 tbsp Garlic (Finely Chopped)

1 tsp Ginger (Finely Chopped)

Spring Onion (Cut Lengthwise)

2-3 Carrots (Peeled & Cut Lengthwise)

1 Bell Pepper/Capsicum (Cut Lengthwise)

1 tbsp Dark Soy Sauce

1 tsp Chili Garlic Paste or Chili Sauce

1 tbsp Tomato Ketchup

1 tsp Pepper Powder

Spring Onion Greens (Garnish)

1 tbsp Oil

Salt to taste

Direction:

1. Heat 1 tbsp Oil in a wok, add the paneer pieces & fry till they turn light brown. Remove & keep it aside

2. In the same wok, add garlic & sauté for 30 seconds.

3. Add ginger & spring onion. Sauté for another 30 seconds on a high flame.

4. Add Carrots & Bell Pepper & sauté for 3-4 minutes.

5. Add Dark Soy Sauce, Chili Sauce, Tomato Ketchup, and Pepper Powder & Salt to taste. Sauté for a minute.
6. Now add the fried Paneer pieces & mix.
7. Add cooked Noodles & mix well.
8. Garnish with Spring Onion greens.

43. Paneer Maggi Noodles

Ingredients

half cup cubed paneer (cottage cheese)
1 packet instant Maggi noodles
1 cup water
1 tsp oil
Little spring onions
Salt to taste (optional)

Direction:
1. How to prepare instant Maggi Noodles
2. Heat oil in a pan and fry the paneer cubes till they turn slightly golden in color.
3. Now remove the paneer from the pan and pour water, bring the water to boil by covering it with a lid.
4. Add the instant Maggi noodles in the boiling water and stir.

5. Time to add spring onions, fried paneer cubes and then add the Maggi tastemaker.
6. Add salt if required.
7. Super easy noodles are ready

44. Crispy Paneer Noodle Fries

Ingredients:

Paneer - 200g cut into medium pieces,
Noodle - 3 cups boiled with salt,
Cornstarch - 4 tbsp,
Lemon juice - 2 tbsp,
Red chili powder - 2 tsp,
Dry fenugreek leaves - 2 tsp,
Turmeric powder - 1/2 tsp,
Garam masala powder - 1 tsp,
Black pepper powder - 1 tsp,
Salt to taste,
Oil for deep fry,

Direction:

1. Take a mixing bowl add Red chili powder, Dry fenugreek leaves, Turmeric powder, Garam masala powder, Black pepper powder and Salt, Mix them with lemon juice.
2. Add Paneer pieces into the masala mixture and coat it nicely. Leave it for 30 minutes.
3. Add Cornstarch to the boiled noodles and mix them well.

4. Wrap the marinated paneer with the noodles and deep-fry it into the medium heat oil.
5. Serve hot.

45. Stir Fry Noodles With Vegetables With Fried Tofu

Ingredients:

1 cup cubed firm tofu

1 tbsp. vegetable oil

1 tsp. vegetable oil

½ cups chopped yellow onion

1 tbsp. chopped garlic

10 cups hot water

1 package tapioca sticks or tapioca rice noodles

3 tbsp. soy sauce

1 tbsp. vegetarian oyster sauce

1 tsp. sugar

3 cups chopped baby bok choy

1 cup sliced mushrooms

1 cup julienned carrots

1 tsp. salt

1 tsp. pepper

½ tsp. mushroom seasoning

Direction:

1. Turn your heat on the medium-high and add in the oil. Fry the tofu on all sides until they turn golden brown. Then remove from the oil and drain on top of paper towels.
2. Add your tapioca sticks into the hot water and allow them to soak for about 30- 40 minutes until they soften.
3. Add the soy sauce, oyster sauce, and sugar into a bowl and stir everything together until the sugar completely dissolves. Then set it aside until it is ready to use.
4. Turn your stove on medium-high heat and add some cooking oil to a large wok or pan.
5. When the oil is hot, add in your garlic and onions and stir-fry them until fragrant.
6. Then add in the vegetables and mix them up.
7. Now add in the soaked tapioca sticks and stir fry everything to combine the ingredients.
8. Pour in your sauce that you made earlier and toss everything up and make sure the sauce coats all of the noodles and vegetables.
9. At this point, if your noodles are too dry, you can add in some water 1 tablespoon at a time to get the noodles to your desired consistency.
10. My noodles were the consistency that I wanted so I did not need to add any water.
11. After stir-frying everything for about 5 minutes, season with salt, pepper and mushroom seasoning.

12. Finally, add in the fried tofu and cook everything up for another minute or until the noodles and vegetables are completely cooked.

Enjoy!

46. Udon Noodle Soup

Ingredients:

3 (7 oz.) packages of udon noodles, or 21 ounces

6 green onions cut on bias

1 package firm tofu, cut into cubes

1 teaspoon toasted sesame oil

1 1/2 tablespoons canola oil

2 tablespoon soy sauce

2 teaspoons sugar

1 tablespoon rice vinegar

Crushed Ginger 1 tbsp.

4 cups broth (chicken, beef, fish, mushroom or vegetable)

Direction:

1. Heat oil in a pan add some sesame oil
2. Fry tofu till golden brown
3. Cook noodles for 10 minutes in a pan by adding water and salt
4. Add crushed ginger on tofu
5. Now add cooked noodles and green onions to the pan mix well and cover with a lid
6. Take a bowl add sugar, soy sauce, and vinegar mix well
7. Add this mixture to the pan

8. Now add 4 cups of chicken broth and salt to the pan mix well

9. Cook for few minutes

10. Delicious noodles are ready. ENJOY!

47. Beef Udon

Ingredients:

1 Tbsp neutral flavor oil (vegetable, canola, etc)

½ Tokyo negi (sub: ½ leek or 2 scallions/green onions)

½ lb thinly sliced beef (chuck or rib eye) (½ = 227 g) (ribeye or top sirloin)

2 packages Udon (I like frozen sanuki noodles)

For Beef

1 Tbsp soy sauce

½-1 Tbsp granulated sugar

For Soup

2 cups dashi (2 cups = 480 ml)

1 Tbsp soy sauce

1 Tbsp mirin

1 tsp granulated sugar

Pinch Kosher salt

For Toppings

Narutomaki (fish cakes) (few slices)

3 sprigs Mitsuba (Japanese parsley) (Optional)

1 green onion/scallion

Shichimi Togarashi (Japanese seven spices) (for taste)

Direction:

1. Gather all the ingredients in a small saucepan; add 2 cups (480 ml) dashi and 1 tsp. sugar.

2. Add 1 Tbsp. mirin and 1 Tbsp. soy sauce and bring it to a boil.

3. Taste the soup and adjust the taste with kosher salt as it will enhance the flavor without adding additional sugar or soy sauce. Cover and keep it on low heat.

4. Cut the Tokyo negi (or use sub) and Narutomaki (fish cake) diagonally.

5. Cut the Mitsuba (optional) into small pieces and thinly slice one onion/scallion (used for topping)

6. Cut the thinly sliced meat into bite size pieces.

7. Bring a big pot of water to a boil. Once boiling, cook the frozen udon for 1 minute. Loosen up the noodles once they started to separate.

8. Once the udon is done cooking, use fine sieve to drain water and transfer to serving bowls

9. While cooking udon, you can start heating the large frying pan. Once it's heated, add 1 Tbsp. vegetable oil and cook the Tokyo negi until tender.

10. Add the meat and brown all sides. Don't move the meat around until it's nicely seared.

11. Once the meat is nicely browned, add ½ to 1 Tbsp. sugar and 1 Tbsp. soy sauce. When the sauce has caramelized and slightly thicken, turn off the heat

12. by this time, the noodle should be in the serving bowls. Pour the hot soup over the udon noodles in the bowls. Then serve the meat on top of the udon noodles.

13. Place the narutomaki (fish cake) and garnish with scallion and mitsuba. If you like it spicy, sprinkle Shichimi Togarashi Enjoy!

48.Chinese Beef Noodle Soup

Ingredients:

10 oz beef shank
8 oz of Chinese wheat noodles
4 Chinese bok choy
1 scallion, sliced
3 ginger, sliced
3 cilantros, chopped
2 dried red peppers
3 cloves of garlic
2 tablespoons of Chinese five-spice powder
3 tablespoons of brown cooking soy sauce
1 tablespoon of chu hou paste
1 tablespoon of dark soy sauce
1 piece of sugar cane
1 tablespoon of shaoxing wine
1 box of beef stock
A pinch of salt
A pinch of sugar
A pinch of white pepper
A dash of sesame oil
4 cups of water

Direction:

1. Blanch the beef in boiling water for 5 minutes to remove extra fat and blood.
2. Take the beef out and allow it to cool for about 5 minutes—it's easier to cut when the beef is cool.
3. Then cut the beef shank in half, and then slice it into 10 pieces.
4. Heat up a pot, add 2 tablespoons of oil, the ginger, scallions, and red peppers, and cook until their aroma comes out.
5. Then add Chu hou paste, brown cooking soy sauce, Shaoxing wine, beef slices, and stir fry for about 20 seconds until everything is coated.
6. Then add 4 cups of water, the dark soy sauce, sugar cane, sesame oil, salt, pepper, and Chinese five-spice powder. Cook for 60 minutes over a low heat.
7. After the braised beef shank is ready, in a separate pot, heat the beef stock, with a pinch of salt, sugar, and white pepper, until boiling.
8. In another pot, boil the noodles in hot water for 5 minutes.
9. Test with chopsticks to see if they break. If they break they are ready.
10. Transfer the noodles to a bowl. Then place the beef and some gravy on top of the noodles.
11. Pour the soup into the bowl. Lastly, garnish with cilantro and scallions.

49. Beef Teriyaki Noodles

Ingredients:

300 gm beef fillet (cut into long strips)
1 large carrot (sliced thin and diagonally)
1 red bell pepper (thinly sliced)
1 onion (thinly sliced)
3 spring onions (sliced)
2 tbsp. cooking oil
125 gm dry egg noodles or fresh egg noodles
½ cup of cold water
3 tbsp. teriyaki sauce
2 tbsp. soy sauce
1 tbsp. sesame oil
½ tsp. ground pepper
½ tsp cornstarch
Coriander to garnish

Direction:

1. In a mixing bowl combine beef, teriyaki sauce, soy sauce, sesame oil and white ground pepper stir well.
2. Add cornstarch mix well with hands.

3. Once the marinade is ready, heat the oil in a pan fry onion on medium heat for 1 minute.

4. Add marinated beef in it fry for 1 minute.

5. Add water and cook for 3 minutes.

6. When the beef is cooking boiled the noodles in another pan or wok

7. Drain the water, separate the noodles and run underneath cold water set aside.

8. Stir the beef in between, once the beef is cooked for 3 minutes add carrot stir, and fry for 30 seconds.

9. Then add bell pepper and spring onion mix and fry all for 30 seconds.

10. Finally, add noodles stir and cook for 1-2 minutes.

11. Garnish with coriander.

50. Uzbek Lagman

Ingredients:

500g of lamb or beef (cubed or thinly sliced)
4-5 medium onions (cut into thin semi circles)
3-4 gloves or chopped garlic
1 medium carrot (thinly sliced)
1 red pepper (thinly sliced/cubed)
2 big tomatoes (cubed)
1 bunch of parsley
150ml of vegetable oil
2 teaspoons of ground coriander
1 teaspoon of anise seeds
1 teaspoon of cumin seed
Black pepper and salt to taste

Directions:

1. Fry the onions with garlic for 10 minutes on medium flame.
2. Add and fry the carrots and pepper for 10 minutes on medium flame.
3. Add the meat and spices and increase the flame to high medium, continue frying for 15-20 minutes by stirring frequently.
4. Add the tomatoes and fry for 10-15 minutes. Stir frequently.

5. Add boiling water and anise seeds. Simmer for 25-30 minutes and it will be ready!

Part 2

Introduction

Pasta can be a wonderful thing, but if you are looking for something on the lighter side, you should consider veggie noodles. Using a Spiralizer, you can turn any vegetable into a fun food. So give these recipes a try and see what you can do with veggie noodles!

Veggie Butternut Squash Noodles With Brown Butter, Sage And Pumpkin Seed Pesto

Ingredients

- 2 medium butternut squash, peeled
- 2 cup loosely packed fresh sage leaves
- 3 tablespoons hulled pumpkin seeds
- ¼ cup good quality Parmesan cheese
- 2 Tablespoons olive oil
- 2 Tablespoons butter
- ¼ cup pomegranate arils
- 2 Tablespoons hulled pumpkin seeds, toasted
- 3 Tablespoons grated Parmesan cheese
- 1 teaspoon ground cinnamon
- Salt & pepper to taste

Directions

1. Cut the butternut squash width-wise, just above the hollow round base of the squash. Keep the round portion for another use. Keep the long, tube-shaped parts of the squash for spiralizing. Use a tabletop spiralizer with a fettuccine attachment to transform the squash into noodle shapes. Set spiralized squash aside.
2. In a blender or food processor combine sage, 3 tablespoons pumpkin seeds and Parmesan cheese. Cover machine and pulse until the mixture resembles course crumbs. With motor running, slowly add in olive oil in a long stream until the

mixture looks like paste. Transfer pesto to a small, airtight container until ready to use.
3. To prepare dish, melt butter over medium heat in a large pan. Add spiralized to pan and toss to coat. Continue cooking over medium heat until squash noodles are tender and butter has browned, about 8 minutes. Add 2-3 tablespoons of the pesto mixture. Toss to combine and continue cooking for 2 minutes more. Season generously with salt and pepper to taste.
4. Remove noodles from heat. Garnish each serving with fresh pomegranate arils, toasted pumpkin seeds, grated Parmesan cheese and a dusting of cinnamon.

Veggie Zucchini Noodles Plus Pancetta And Parmesan

Ingredients

- 4-5 green and yellow zucchinis, washed and ends trimmed
25 grams pancetta, cut into cubes
1 garlic clove, minced
1 shallot, minced
1/3 cup finely grated parmesan cheese
big pinch black pepper
chopped parsley for garnish

Directions

1. using your spiralizer, spiralize zucchinis into long noodles. place in a colander over a bowl and toss with about 1/2 teaspoon or so of salt. let rest for 30 minutes. this will draw out some of the moisture from the zucchinis.
2. heat some olive oil in a large pan over medium heat, and add the pancetta. fry until crispy and the whites of the fat have disappeared. add garlic and shallots, and cook until soft and fragrant.
3. while the garlic and shallot is cooking, squeeze the remaining moisture out of the noodles with a paper towel, then add to the pan. cook over medium heat for about 3-5 minutes, until noodles are getting crisp-tender. add the cheese and black pepper and cook for another minute or so more, until cheese melts and coats the noodles.

4. remove from heat and place in bowls, sprinkling parsley over top. enjoy!

Veggie Noodle With Avocado, Tomato And Pine Nut Courgetti

Ingredients

- 55g (1/3 cup) pine nuts
- 1 leek, only the white part
- Olive oil
- 1 large avocado, stoned and peeled
- 1 garlic clove
- drizzle of extra virgin olive oil
- salt and pepper
- 1 tbsp lemon juice
- 14 cherry tomatoes, halved
- About 475g courgette, spiralized or ribbons created with a peeler (2-3 large courgettes)
- A handful of grated parmesan, or dairy-free alternative if vegetarian/vegan

Directions

1. Heat a frying pan on a med-high heat and once hot, toast the pine nuts in the pan, stirring frequently with a wooden spoon. Once they have turned golden brown and start to smell more nutty, remove from the heat and pour into a small bowl for later, do this immediately as they will quickly burn.
2. Chop the end root off the leek, then slice into 2 where it starts to turn green, you only need the white part for this recipe. Peel back the first few outer layers of the white part of the leek and

discard. Slice the leek into small rounds. Add 1/2 tsp of olive oil to the frying pan and heat, saute the leek until soft, about 5 minutes. Then transfer to a small bowl/plate.
3. To make the avocado sauce, put the green flesh of the avocado in a food processor, along with a peeled garlic clove, a drizzle of extra virgin olive oil, seasoning to taste and the lemon juice. Blitz till a smooth, creamy consistency, taste and adjust seasoning or add more olive oil if you want it less thick.
4. Heat the frying pan on a high heat, add another 1/2 tsp of olive oil and add the halved cherry tomatoes, once they start to colour on the edges and the skin shrivels add the spiralized courgette to the hot pan and continually stir, cook for a further 3-4 minutes. You don't want to cook the courgette too much, or else they will be too soft and release a lot of water.
5. Remove the pan from the heat and pour into a big serving bowl. Drizzle over the avocado sauce, with the sauteed leek. Stir to coat everything, then sprinkle over the toasted pine nuts and a grating of parmesan or alternative.
6. Best eaten straight away as the avocado in the sauce will slowly turn brown.

Veggie Paleo Celeriac Carbonara Casserole

Ingredients

- ½ cup raw cashew nuts
- 1 tablespoon coconut oil or olive oil
- 1 medium brown onion, finely diced
- 6 rashers/streaks of bacon (middle bacon/Canadian bacon, pancetta is also great), diced into small cubes
- 2 medium cloves of garlic, finely diced
- 1 teaspoon sea salt
- ½ teaspoon white or black pepper
- 1 tablespoon butter or ghee (or extra olive oil)
- 1 large celeriac, peeled and spiralized into ribbons
- 3 eggs
- ½ cup almond milk
- 2 tablespoons nutritional yeast flakes
- Chopped parsley to serve

Directions

1. Add the cashew nuts to a bowl and cover with warm water. Allow to soak for 15-20 minutes.
2. Preheat the oven to 200 C / 395 F.
3. In a large frying pan, heat a tablespoon of olive oil or coconut oil over medium-high heat. Add the bacon and pan-fry for 3 minutes, stirring a few times.
4. Add the onion to the bacon and pan-fry together, stirring a few times, for 5 minutes. Once softened,

add the garlic, salt, pepper and butter (or ghee) and stir through for 20 more seconds.
5. While the bacon and onions are cooking, prepare the celeriac. Cut off the hard ends from the celeriac root and peel the sides. Depending on the type of vegetable spiralizer you use (I use Paderno spiralizer), you might need to cut the celeriac in two halves as it can be a little difficult to spiralize the whole root at once. I cut mine in two halves and trimmed the ends so their are flat. Spiralize each half into noodle ribbons and set aside. See cook's notes for more on how to spiralize it.
6. Transfer the celeriac noodles and the cooked bacon and onions mixture to a large mixing bowl.
7. Strain the cashews and add to a blender or a food processor together with the eggs (whites and yolks), almond milk and nutritional yeast flakes. Add another pinch of salt and process for 30 seconds until smooth (it's okay if some of the cashews are not completely pulverised, adds a bit of texture).
8. Pour the egg mixture over the celeriac noodles. Using your hands, mix everything together working the sauce through the noodles. Transfer to a round or square casserole dish and place in the oven, middle shelf for 12 minutes.
9. Once you remove the casserole dish, the celeriac should be crisped up and golden brown on the top. The egg mixture would have cooked firmer around the edges of the dish and on the bottom, yet will

still be a little creamy in the middle. Serve with chopped up parsley on the side.

Veggie Noodle Curry Butternut Squash

Ingredients

Curry Sauce:

- 1/2 teaspoon fresh Ginger, grated
- 2 garlic cloves. Mined
- Red pepper flakes
- 1 teaspoon cumin
- 1 tablespoon green curry paste, *see notes
- 2 cups full fat coconut milk
- 2 teaspoons lime juice, more to taste
- 1 teaspoon fish sauce
- 1 teaspoon coconut sugar
- 1/4 teaspoon sea salt, more to taste

Other Ingredients:

- 1 large butternut squash (about 3 cups noodles)
- 1 red pepper, thinly sliced
- 1 green pepper, thinly sliced
- 1 yellow onion, thinly sliced
- 1/4 teaspoon sea salt
- 1 tablespoon scallions, thinly sliced
- 1 tablespoon cilantro, for garnish
- 1 lime, sliced into wedges for garnish
- 1 red chili pepper, sliced thin for garnish
- Optional: 1cup fresh spinach

Directions

1. Make the Sauce: Heat ginger, garlic, red pepper flakes, cumin, and green curry paste on medium

heat for 1 minutes. Add coconut milk, lime juice, fish sauce, coconut sugar and sea salt. Whisk to combine. Bring sauce ingredients to a boil over medium-high heat. Once at a boil, lower the heat to low, and let simmer for 10-15 minutes. Taste and adjust seasoning as desired.
2. Heat 2 teaspoons extra-virgin olive oil in a large sauté pan. Add peppers, onions, and sea salt.
3. Sauté until onions turn translucent and the peppers have started to softened, about 3-5 minutes. Add butternut squash and sauté for an additional 5-7 minutes. If adding the spinach, add at the end and toss until wilted.
4. Place butternut zoodles, peppers, and onions in a large serving bowl. Pour curry sauce over the veggies. Garnish with cilantro, scallions, and red chili pepper if using. Serve warm!

Notes

- This dish isn't very spicy, but has a kick. If you don't like spicy food, start with 1/4 teaspoon green curry paste and add more to taste while the sauce is cooking!
- You can add any veggies to this dish that you have on hand! Potatoes, carrots, corn, spinach, etc. If you add vegetables, add them along with the peppers and onions with the exception of dark leafy greens such as spinach and kale. Add the leafy greens once the butternut squash has cooked for at least 5 minutes and cook the leafy green just until it starts

to wilt. If added before, the greens will be overcooked.

Veggie Rainbow Noodle Salad

Ingredients

- 2 small beets, peeled & spiralized on medium setting
- 1 medium zucchini, spiralized on medium setting
- 2 large carrots, spiralized on medium setting
- 1 Granny Smith apple, spiralized on medium setting
- 1/2 avocado, sliced or diced
- 1/4 cup chopped peanuts
- 1/2 tablespoon chives, chopped
- Sesame seeds (optional, for garnish)
- Lime wedges (optional, for garnish)

Dressing:

- 1 teaspoon soy sauce
- 1/4 cup sesame oil
- 1 teaspoon rice vinegar
- Juice from 1/2 lime
- 1/4 cup water
- 1 clove garlic, minced
- 1 teaspoon brown sugar
- 1/2 avocado

Directions

1. Add all dressing ingredients to a blender and blend until combined. Set aside.
2. Add the rest of the ingredients to a large bowl and gently toss with the dressing. Serve immediately.

Veggie Chive Oil Zucchini Noodles With Roasted Tofu

Ingredients

For Chive OIl

- 1 cup canola oil
- 2 oz fresh onion chives, cut into 1.5-inch segments
- For Zucchini Noodles
- 2 medium size (1 lb 3 oz) zucchini squashes
- 1 lb extra firm tofu, cubed

For Roasted Tofu

- 2 teaspoons canola oil
- 1 lb extra firm tofu
- ⅛ teaspoon salt
- ⅛ teaspoon black pepper

For Sauce

- 1½ tablespoons chive oil (see directions below)
- 1 tablespoon gluten-free soy sauce
- 1 teaspoon erythritol or coconut sugar
- ¼ teaspoon salt

Garnish

- 2 teaspoons chopped chives
- 1 pinch roasted sesame seeds

Directions

1. To make the chive oil: Heat oil in a saucepan over medium heat. Add onion chives into the saucepan until the oil is hot, but not smoky hot. Stir briefly.

Reduce the heat to medium-low and let the chives simmer in oil without cover on for 20 minutes. Watch occasionally to make sure the oil is not too hot to avoid burning the chives. The chives should be dark greenish brown instead of black when the chive oil is ready.
2. To make the roasted tofu: Preheat oven to 425 °F. Heat 2 teaspoons of canola oil in a skillet over high heat until the oil is hot. Add tofu cubes and fry until all sides turn slightly brown. Transfer the tofu cubes onto a baking sheet and roast in oven for 20 minutes until they are golden brown. Sprinkle salt and pepper to taste.
3. Let the chive oil cool slightly. Combine all the sauce ingredients and mix well in a small mixing bowl.
4. Use a spiralizer to make zucchini noodles.
5. Toss the sauce and zucchini noodles together. Garnish with fresh chopped chives and roasted sesame. Serve with roasted tofu immediately.

Veggie Noodle Sauteed Zucchini Ribbions

Ingredients

- 1/2 red bell pepper
- 1 carrot
- 2 zucchini, 3 if they are on the smaller side
- 1 Tbsp olive oil
- 1/4 tsp salt
- 1/3 C canned peas
- 1/3 C mayo
- 1 Tbsp yellow mustard
- 1/2 tsp pepper

Directions

1. Finely dice bell pepper and carrots. Spiralize the zucchini using a ribbon blade (alternatively, you can use a julienne peeler or a sharp knife to carefully slice into noodle sized strips.)
2. Heat olive oil in a skillet over medium heat. Once hot, toss the zucchini and 1/4 tsp salt in the olive oil using tongs. Saute until zucchini is just barely softened (about 2 minutes) while using tongs to continually stir.
3. Transfer zucchini to a paper towel lined plate to drain any excess water/oil and cool a bit.
4. Stir together the bell pepper, carrots, peas, mayo, and mustard. Add zucchini and black pepper then use tongs to toss everything together until well-combined. Best served chilled.

Veggie Noodle With Sweet Potato And Spicy Pepita Gremolata

Ingredients

- 1/4 cup pepitas, roughly chopped
- zest of one lemon
- 1/3 cup Italian flat-leaf parsley, chopped
- 1 tsp fresh garlic, finely minced (1-2 cloves)
- a dash of cayenne pepper, to taste
- a big pinch of salt
- 2 large sweet potatoes, peeled
- 2-3 T olive oil
- salt, to taste

Directions

1. Mix all the gremolata ingredients together and set aside.
2. Use a spiralizer to turn the sweet potatoes into noodles. (See above for some additional spiralizer/noodle tips.)
3. Pour olive oil into a large pan on medium-high heat.
4. Once the oil is hot enough to sizzle, add the sweet potato noodles in a single layer, turning gently as needed. You may need to cook them in smaller batches to make sure they cook evenly.
5. After about 7 minutes in the pan, they should be tender but not so soft that they are falling apart. Sprinkle with salt.
6. Serve the noodles warm with a heap of gremolata spooned on top (you might have some gremolata

leftover — put it on anything!). If it's not spicy enough for you, top with a shake or two of crushed red pepper.

Veggie Noodles One-Pot Healthy Pasta

Ingredients

- 1 tablespoon of olive oil
- 2 8-ounce boneless skinless chicken breasts
- 2 cups of sliced asparagus stalks
- 1 cup of peas
- 4 each spiralized green zucchini and yellow squash
- 3 cups of sliced assorted tomatoes
- ½ cup of vegetable stock
- 1 cup of ciliegine mozzarella
- ½ cup of bread crumbs
- ¼ cup of shredded parmesan cheese
- Fresh basil leaves and sliced green onions for garnish
- Kosher salt and fresh cracked pepper to taste

Directions

1. Heat the olive oil in very large sauté pan over high heat and add in the chicken breasts. Season the chicken with salt and pepper once it's in the pan.
2. Flip the chicken over after 3 to 4 minutes or until it's golden brown, turn the heat to medium-high, and season the other side with salt and pepper. Continue to cook until the chicken is cooked throughout, about 7 to 8 minutes.
3. Remove the chicken from the pan.
4. Add the asparagus, peas, zucchini and squash to the hot pan and saute for 3 to 4 minutes or until the veggies become lightly browned.

5. Next, add in the tomatoes and vegetable stock and cook for a further 3 to 4 minutes over high heat.
6. Season everything with salt and pepper and transfer the mixture to a large bowl.
7. Slice the chicken and add it to the top of the pasta along with the mozzarella, bread crumbs, parmesan cheese, basil leaves and sliced green onions.

Veggie Noodle Teriyaki Chicken

Ingredients

- 2-3 boneless, skinless chicken breasts, cut into bite-size pieces
- 1 tablespoon olive oil
- 2 medium zucchini, spiralized on medium setting
- 1 tablespoon cornstarch + 2 tablespoons cold water
- Scallions, chopped, to taste (optional)

Teriyaki sauce:

- 2 tablespoons (packed) brown sugar
- 2 tablespoons soy sauce
- 2 tablespoons honey
- 1 clove garlic, minced
- 2 tablespoons water
- Pepper, to taste

Directions

1. Prep your chicken. Add it to a large skillet along with the olive oil. Stir until chicken is coated. Cook over medium-high heat, stirring often, for 5-7 minutes, or until it's cooked through (don't overcook).

2. Meanwhile, spiralize your zucchini and set aside. Add the teriyaki sauce ingredients to a small bowl and whisk together. Also get your cornstarch mixture ready in another small bowl and chop the scallions if using.
3. When the chicken is about done, reduce the heat to medium and add the teriyaki sauce mixture and the cornstarch mixture to the skillet. Stir well so the chicken is coated, and let it bubble (it will thicken fast) for a minute or two.
4. Add the zucchini noodles to the skillet and using tongs, toss them with the teriyaki chicken. The zucchini will release water. Don't cook the zoodles for too long or they will get limp and watery. I warm them through for a couple of minutes max, tossing continuously.
5. Serve immediately with scallions sprinkled over top if desired. Enjoy!

Veggie Noodles With Spinach, Bacon, Mushroom And Sweet Potato

Ingredients

- 4 slices bacon, chopped
- 8oz mushrooms, sliced
- 1 small shallot, minced
- 1 large sweet potato (1lb), peeled then spiralized with the smallest noodle blade
- 2 cloves garlic, pressed or minced
- 1/4 cups gluten-free chicken broth
- 4 cups loosely packed baby spinach, roughly chopped
- salt and pepper
- 3-4 eggs

Directions

1. Add bacon to a large, 12" skillet over medium high heat. Saute until browned then scoop onto a plate and set aside. Leave bacon grease in skillet.
2. Turn heat up to medium-high then add mushrooms and shallots to the bacon grease. Saute until mushrooms have released their liquid and begin to turn golden brown, 4-5 minutes. Add sweet potato noodles then saute, gently tossing with tongs, until the noodles are nearly al dente, 5 minutes - adding an extra drizzle of extra virgin olive oil and/or turning the heat down slightly if necessary to avoid burning the sweet potatoes. Add garlic then saute for 30 more seconds.

3. Add spinach and chicken broth to the skillet then saute until the sweet potato noodles are tender, 2-3 minutes. Taste then add salt and pepper if necessary.
4. Place a lid partially on top of the skillet to keep noodles warm then cook eggs according to your preference in a small skillet.
5. Scoop sweet potato noodles onto plates then top with eggs and cooked bacon.

Noodle Recipes

1) Soba Noodle Soup

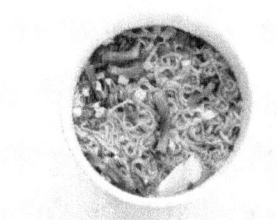

This recipe uses an instant bonito flavored soup base which will save you time and you won't have to prepare dashi from scratch. Soba noodles are chewy and thick. You can also use hard-boiled egg and scallion as this soup's topping.

Serving Sizes: **1**

Cooking Time: **10 minutes**

List of Ingredients:

- Soba noodles, 1 bundle
- Fresh mushrooms, 3
- Water, 1 ½ cups
- Carrots, 3, sliced
- Bonito flavored soup base, 2 tbsp.

- Peas, 3
- Shrimps, 3, shelled and deveined

For Toppings:

- Seaweed strips, ½, thinly sliced, toasted
- Togarashi

Procedure:

Fill a pot with water and add soba noodles and boil for 5 minutes. Rinse and drain. Keep aside.

Boil 1 ½ cup of water and stir the soup base. Combine well.

Now add the remaining ingredients and cook for 4 minutes or until shrimps are well cooked.

Transfer noodles in a serving bowl and pour the soup on top.

Garnish with togarashi and nori strips.

2) Chanpon Noodles

Chanpon noodles are a quick fix version of ramen made with few ingredients and in no time. The soup base is made with strong flavors of oyster sauce, mirin, ramen stock and soy sauce. Spicy kimchi sauce and tobanjan chili are added to jazz up the flavor. If you like extra heat, then sprinkle a tsp. of chili pepper and oil.

Serving Sizes: **2**

Cooking Time: **30 minutes**

List of Ingredients:
- Champon noodles, 150g
- Large prawns, 4
- Spring onion, 2, chopped
- Kamaboko, 4 thin slices
- Sliced squid, 25g
- Carrot, 1, sliced
- Pork, 40g, thinly sliced

- Cabbage, 60g, chopped
- Bean sprouts, 50g
- Salt, to taste
- Pepper, to pepper

For Soup:

- Oyster sauce, 2 tbsp.
- Ramen stock soup, 3 tbsp.
- Soy sauce, 2 tbsp.
- Korean tobanjan chili, 1 tsp.
- Water
- Spicy kimchi sauce, 2 tbsp.
- Mirin, 2 tbsp.
- Ginger paste, 1 tbsp.

For Toppings:

- Corn
- Chili pepper, to taste
- Korean tobanjan chili, 1 tsp.
- Chili oil, to taste

Procedure:

Fill a stock pot with water and add all the soup ingredients. Bring the mixture to a boil.

Reduce the heat and simmer for 8 minutes. Remove from heat and keep aside.

Heat 1 tbsp. of oil in saucepan and add pork, prawns and squids. Cook thoroughly.

Now add kamaboko slices and veggies. Season with salt and pepper.

Pour soup in the cooking meat and stir well. Allow it to simmer for 5 minutes.

Now add noodles and allow them to cook in the soup.

Divide soup into 2 serving bowls and top it with spring onion, corn, Korean chili and sprinkle chili pepper.

3) Hakata Ramen

This recipe is a Japanese classic. The length of the ingredients list may seem a little long but the preparation process is very simple. Make sure you prepare the toppings before preparing the noodles as these noodles require only 30 seconds and needs to be served immediately.

Serving Sizes: **4**

Cooking Time: **15 minutes**

List of Ingredients:

For the Soup:
- Water, 6 cups
- Sake, 2 tbsp.
- Green onions, 1 bunch
- Sesame oil, 1 tsp.
- Ginger root, 50g, sliced
- Soy sauce, 4 tbsp.

- Salt, 1 tsp.
- Garlic, 3 cloves, skinned

For the Meat:

- Pork, 1 pound
- Salt, 1 tsp.

For the Noodles:

- Fresh angel hair pasta, 9 oz.
- Baking soda, 2 tbsp.
- Water, 8 cups

For the Toppings:

- Green onions, chopped
- Boiled eggs, halved
- Bean sprouts, blanched briefly

Procedure:

Rub salt on pork and refrigerate for 12 hours at least.

To prepare soup bring water to a boil with pork, onions, ginger, and garlic. Once it starts boiling you will notice scum forming on top. Remove it and cover the lid. Turn the heat low and allow it to simmer for 2 hours.

Strain the mixture and reserve pork. Slice it and keep aside.

Again bring the broth to a boil and stir sake and soy sauce. Season with salt and add sesame oil,

Simmer on low heat and cook noodles in the meantime.

Put a clean pot on heat and fill it with water. Add baking powder.

Stir noodles and cook for no longer than 30 seconds.

Divide noodles into 4 serving bowls and pour simmering soup on top.

Add green onions, egg and bean sprout.

Serve hot.

4) Miso Ramen

The toppings of miso ramen are varied therefore you have plenty of options to choose from. You can also top miso ramen with ramen egg, shiraga negi, spicy bean sprout salad or chashu. Remember not to add salt while preparing the noodles as the noodle batter already contains enough salt.

Serving Sizes: **2**

Cooking Time: **25 minutes**

List of Ingredients:

- Ramen noodles, 2 packages
- Sesame oil, 1 tbsp.
- White pepper, ¼ tsp.
- Garlic, 2 cloves, minced
- Sake, 1 tbsp.
- Sesame seeds, 1 tbsp., grinded
- Salt, 1 tsp.
- Sugar, 1 tbsp.
- Shallot, 1, finely chopped
- Chicken broth, 4 cups
- Miso, 3 tbsp.
- Chili bean sauce, 2 tsp.
- Ginger, 1 inch piece, minced
- Ground pork, ¼ pound

For topping:

- Nori (seaweed)
- Scallions, chopped
- Corn kernels
- La-yu (Japanese chili oil)
- Pickled red ginger

Procedure:

Heat oil and sauté ginger, shallots and garlic until aromatic.

Add ground pork and cook on medium-high heat until the meat is no longer pink.

Start seasoning and add miso, sugar, sake, bean paste, sesame seeds, salt and pepper.

Stir broth and combine well.

Reduce the heat and simmer for 10-15 minutes.

Prepare noodles according to the package directions.

Transfer cooked noodles to individual bowls and pour soup on top.

Serve with pickled ginger, corns, scallions, nori and Japanese chili oil.

5) Coconut Lime Noodle Soup

In the scorching heat of summer this coconut lime soup comes as bliss. The flavors are exotic with hotness of tograshi, saltiness of fish sauce, sweetness of sugar and tanginess of lime juice. You can also use udon noodles for this recipe if you don't have soba or ramen.

Serving Sizes: **4**

Cooking Time: **15 minutes**

List of Ingredients:
- Chicken broth, 32 oz.
- Soba/chukamen noodles, ¾ pound
- Coconut milk, 1 can of 13.5 oz.
- Lime juice, 6 tbsp.
- Ginger, 2 inch piece sliced into ¼ inch thick pieces
- Shrimps, 8, shelled and deveined
- Tograshi, 1 tbsp.

- Chicken breast, 1 pound, boneless and skinless, thinly sliced
- Light brown sugar, 2 tsp.
- Fish sauce, 3 tbsp.
- Cilantro leaves, ¾ cup

Procedure:

Prepare noodles according to the package directions.

Fill a stock pot with chicken broth and add ginger. Bring it to a boil. Reduce the heat and simmer for 15 minutes.

Stir coconut milk and stir well. Add seafood and meat and simmer until it is thoroughly cooked.

Season with sugar, togarashi, fish sauce, and lime juice,

Add ½ cup cilantro followed by noodles. Mix well.

Ladle into a serving bowl and garnish with remaining cilantro.

6) Shrimp Noodle Soup

If you have some leftover shrimps from last night then this is a delicious way to put them to use. Ramen noodles and a few sauces is all that is required to prepare this easy and simple soup. Make sure you only add 2 seasoning packets from the noodles otherwise you will end up having salty soup.

Serving Sizes: **6**

Cooking Time: **25 minutes**

List of Ingredients:

- Chicken flavor ramen noodles, 4 packages, half torn
- Shrimp, 8 oz. medium sized, deveined and peeled
- Carrots, 2, sliced
- Lime zest of 1 lime
- Fresh basil, 1 tsp., chopped
- Green onions, 3, chopped

- Ginger, 2 tbsp., peeled and silvered
- Mushrooms, 1 cup, sliced
- Thai hot chili sauce, 1 tbsp.
- Lime juice from 1 lime
- Spinach, 2 cups, chopped
- Garlic, 2 cloves, minced
- Water, 8 cups
- Fish sauce/soy sauce, 2 tbsp.

Procedure:

Boil water in a pot.

Add carrots, basil, green onion, ginger, chili sauce, garlic and fish sauce.

Add 2 packets of ramen noodle seasoning and bring to a boil.

Reduce the heat and simmer for 10 minutes.

Now add mushrooms, noodles, shrimps and spinach. Simmer for another 10 minutes.

Lastly add lime juice and zest and combine well.

Transfer to a serving bowl and enjoy.

7) Udon Miso Noodle Soup

This recipe can also be jazzed up by using different vegetables like zucchini, corn, cabbage or broccoli florets. Just slice all the vegetables thinly and add in the simmering soup and cook until tender. If you don't have white miso then you can also use another type of miso but make sure to check for flavors.

Serving Sizes: **4**

Cooking Time: **10 minutes**

List of Ingredients:
- Fresh udon noodles, 1 package of 12 oz.
- White miso, 2 tbsp.
- Carrots, ½ cup, thinly sliced
- Vegetable/chicken stock, 4 cups
- Fresh mushrooms, ½ cup
- Green onions, ½ cup

- Snow peas, ½ cup, cut diagonally

Procedure:

Prepare noodles according to the directions on package. Rinse and drain. Keep aside.

Fill a stock pot with stock and bring it to a boil.

Reduce the heat and add carrots. Cook for 2 minutes then add peas and cook for another 2 minutes. Lastly add mushrooms and cook for 30 seconds.

Remove the pot from heat.

Fill a medium bowl with miso and stir 1 tbsp. of simmering soup. Stir to dissolve well.

Transfer miso to the pot and give it a good stir.

Add noodles and garnish with green onions.

Serve.

8) Sweet Red Chili Noodles With Sesame Seeds

This sweet and spicy recipe is very easy to make and is an excellent snack. All you have to do is combine four ingredients together and you are all set. You can also refrigerate any leftovers and reheat in the microwave the next day.

Serving Sizes: **4**

Cooking Time: **15 minutes**

List of Ingredients:
- Noodles, 16 oz.
- Sesame seeds, 2 tbsp.
- Sweet red chili sauce, ¼ cup
- Lime juice, 2 tbsp.
- Olive oil, 2 tbsp.

Procedure:

Combine chili sauce with sesame seeds, lime juice and olive oil.

Cook noodles according to the package directions.

Divide noodles between four bowls equally and add sauce. Combine well and serve.

9) Tsuke-Men Noodles

Tsukemen noodles are also known as dipping noodles. These belong to the family of cold noodles and are served separately with simmering soup and various toppings. The soup base is mainly made with soy sauce and mirin. You can add any type of topping you want to these noodles for example, mushrooms, cabbage and scallion.

Serving Sizes: **2**

Cooking Time: **15 minutes**

List of Ingredients:

- Soy sauce, ¼ cup
- Fresh chukamen noodles, 2 packages
- Mirin, 2 tbsp.
- Chicken soup stock, 2/3 cup
- Japanese rice vinegar, 1 tsp.

For Toppings:

- Cucumber, thinly sliced
- Green onion, 1, chopped
- Boiled eggs, 2, cut into halves
- Nori seaweed, 1 sheet sliced thinly
- Tomatoes, 1, cut into cubes
- Ham, sliced
- Lettuce, torn into small pieces

Procedure:

Combine chicken stock, mirin and soy sauce together in a pot and bring it to a boil.

Turn the heat off and stir vinegar.

Fill another pot with water and boil noodles. Rinse and drain.

Fill a large bowl with ice water and place noodles bowl into it so that the noodles cool down quickly.

Now divide cold noodles into 2 individual serving bowls. Also transfer the soup into 2 different serving bowls. Arrange 2 plates with the toppings and serve.

10) Sirloin-Snap Pea Stir-Fry

Stir-frying meat and veggies is one of the best ways to cook them. It helps retain the true flavors and nutrition of the meat and veggies. This recipe also saves a lot of your time and is ready within 15 minutes.

Serving Sizes: **4**

Cooking Time: **25 minutes**

List of Ingredients:
- Buckwheat noodles
- Ginger, ¼ cup, chopped
- Beef broth, 1 cup
- Garlic, 3 cloves, smashed
- Sugar snap peas, 1 pound
- Scallions, 6, chopped
- Cornstarch, 2 tbsp.
- Vegetable oil, 3 tbsp.
- Soy sauce, ¼ cup

- Toasted sesame oil, 1 tbsp.
- Sirloin steak, 1 pound, boneless and cut crosswise

Procedure:

Cook noodles in boiling water. Strain and keep aside.

Boil peas for 2 minutes. Strain and keep aside.

Heat 1 tbsp. of vegetable oil and stir-fry sirloin for 5 minutes. Transfer to a paper towel.

Stir-fry scallions, ginger and garlic in the remaining vegetable oil for 2 minutes.

In a medium bowl combine broth with cornstarch and soy sauce.

Stir it with the scallions, ginger and garlic and cook for 1 minute.

Now add meat and peas. Drizzle sesame oil and add noodles.

Toss well and transfer to a serving bowl.

11) Fried Ramen Soup

Have you ever considered frying up your bowl of ramen soup? If not then give this fried ramen soup recipe a shot and be amazed by the delicious outcome. The crunchy, crispy and fried noodles are more scrumptious than the classic soup itself.

Serving Sizes: **1**

Cooking Time: **5 minutes**

List of Ingredients:

- Ramen noodles, 1 packet
- Oil for frying

Procedure:

Heat oil in a shallow pan.

Break ramen into medium size pieces. DONOT crumble them.

Deep fry the noodles until golden and crisp.

Transfer on a paper towel to drain excess oil.

Dust the seasoning mix and toss it well to combine.

Enjoy!

12) Sapporo Ramen

This recipe of sapporo ramen is made with the base of chicken broth flavored with white and brown miso paste, dried seaweed and mushrooms. It is topped with mighty slices of spicy chashu and butter and marinated soft-boiled eggs.

Serving Sizes: **4**

Cooking Time: **50 minutes**

List of Ingredients:

- Fresh ramen noodles, 400g
- Nori sheets, sliced into strips
- Bamboo shoots, 1 can of 200g, drained
- Corns from 1 cob
- Sesame oil, to serve
- Bean sprouts, 1 ¼ cups
- Butter, cut into 4 blocks
- Spring onions, 2, cut diagonally
- Dried chili flakes, to serve

For Chashu Pork:

- Pork belly, boneless, 500g
- Spring onions, 4, chopped
- Sake, ¼ cup
- Soy sauce, ½ cup
- Garlic, 6 cloves, bruised
- Caster sugar, ¼ cup
- Mirin, 1 cup
- Ginger, 1 inch piece, sliced

For Chicken Stock:

- Chicken bones, 1 pound
- Dried seaweed, 2 pieces
- Brown miso paste, ¼ cup
- Leek, 1, white part only, chopped
- White miso paste, ¼ cup
- Ginger, ½ inch piece, sliced
- Shiitake mushrooms, 1/3 cup

For Soft Boiled Eggs:

- Soft-boiled eggs, 4, peeled
- Soy sauce, ½ cup
- Caster sugar, 1 tsp.

Procedure:

Start off by cooking chashu. Preheat the oven to 140 F.

Wrap pork belly with a kitchen string leaving 3cm space after each roll.

Fill a large casserole with water and stir soy sauce, sake and mirin. Add sugar, onions, garlic and ginger.

When the sugar has dissolved completely, boil the mixture on high heat.

Now add pork and cover the lid.

Place the dish into the oven and cook for 3 hours. You need to cook the meat until it's completely cooked and tender.

When done slice the meat and keep it aside.

To prepare eggs, combine soy sauce, water and sugar together.

Add soft-boiled eggs and cover the bowl. Place it in the refrigerator for 3 hours.

To prepare stock, fill a large stock pot with water and add chicken, mushrooms, ginger, seaweed and leek. Bring it to a boil.

Now simmer on low heat for 1 ½ hours, discarding the scum occasionally.

Strain the stock in a large bowl. Transfer the liquid back to the pot and stir brown and white miso paste. Mix well.

Now prepare noodles according to the directions. Rinse and drain.

Fill each serving bowl with noodles and add simmering stock. Top it with sliced pork, nori strips, corns, butter, bean sprouts, spring onions, bamboo shoots and marinated eggs.

Sprinkle some sesame oil and chili flakes.

Serve.

13) Tan Tan Ramen Noodles

Tantan-Men is the Japanese version of dan dan noodles, typically made in pork broth and are seasoned with soy sauce, sesame and chili oil. The hearty pork slices makes this dish a perfect main course that is delicious and filling at the same time.

Serving Sizes: **2**

Cooking Time: **15 minutes**

List of Ingredients:

For the soup:

- Ramen noodles, 7 oz.
- Soy sauce, 3 tbsp.
- Sesame oil, 2 tsp.
- Rice vinegar, 2 tsp.
- Pork broth, 3 cups
- Layu chili oil, 2 tsp.

- Tahini sesame paste, 4 tbsp.
- Garlic, 2 cloves, chopped

For Topping:

- Minced pork, 400g
- Spinach, 1 cup, chopped
- Sake, 4 tsp.
- Spring onions, 3, chopped
- Soy sauce, 2 tbsp.
- Tenmenjan sweet bean sauce, 2 tbsp.

Procedure:

Marinate minced pork with cooking sake and keep aside for 15 minutes.

Heat 1 tbsp. oil in a pan and cook marinated meat until browned.

Stir soy sauce and tenmenjan and combine well. When the meat has cooked through, remove from heat and keep aside.

In the same pan sauté garlic until fragrant.

Transfer sautéed garlic into the individual serving bowls. Pour rice vinegar, sesame oil, layu, sake, tahini and soy sauce. Keep aside.

Fill a stock pot with water and broth. Add spinach and bring the mixture to a boil. Reduce the heat and simmer until the spinach wilts.

Cook noodles in another pot for 5 minutes. Drain.

Now divide simmer broth among the individual serving bowls.

Add noodles and top with spinach, seasoned pork mince and spring onions.

Serve.

14) Yakisoba Noodle Stir Fry

This recipe is a blend of sweet and spicy flavors with balanced sourness and saltiness. To enhance flavors you can add garlic and lime zest to the sauce. You can eat noodle stir fry with steak for a filling meal.

Serving Sizes: **2**

Cooking Time: **15 minutes**

List of Ingredients:

- Yakisoba noodles, 2 packages of 5.6 oz.
- Scallions, 2, chopped
- Red pepper flakes, 1/8 tsp.
- Soy sauce, ¼ cup
- Shredded cabbage, 1 cup
- Rice vinegar, ¼ cup
- White sugar, 1 tbsp.
- Onion, 1 small, sliced vertically
- Vegetable/chicken broth, ¼ cup
- Vegetable oil, 1 tbsp.

Procedure:

Prepare soba noodles according to the directions.

To prepare sauce mix soy sauce with vinegar, sugar and pepper. Stir water and combine well.

Sauté onions for 1 minute then add cabbage and stir fry for 3 minutes.

Add sauce and cook for 1 minute.

Add prepared noodles and stir-fry for 5 minutes while tossing.

Transfer to a serving bowl and garnish with scallions and serve.

15) Sesame Ramen Noodles

Sesame ramen noodles recipe are a basic base recipe that compliments all kinds of sautéed veggies and stir-fry. You can top these basic seasoned noodles with your favorite veggies, meat or seafood. These noodles can also be used as a salad or a proper main course if tossed with meat and sauce.

Serving Sizes: **2**

Cooking Time: **5 minutes**

List of Ingredients:

- Ramen noodles, 1 package, any flavor
- Sesame seeds, 1 tbsp.
- Sesame oil, 2 tsp.

Procedure:

Fill a pot with water and break noodle brick in half. Add it to the boiling water and cook for 3 minutes. Do not add the seasoning mix.

Drain and rinse well.

Place the noodles back in the same pot and sprinkle sesame seeds and drizzle sesame oil. Toss well to combine.

Mix with the veggies of your choice and enjoy.

16) Hiyashi Chuka

This is a cold noodles dish served with different toppings for varied flavor, giving it a colorful kick. You can also add additional toppings for example, bean sprouts, ham and tomatoes. Typically this dish uses Japanese rice vinegar for dressing but you can also use soy sauce or sesame oil, what you have available.

Serving Sizes: **4**

Cooking Time: **15 minutes**

List of Ingredients:

- Chukamen noodles, 4 packages
- Eggs, 2, beaten
- Chicken breasts, ¼ pound, sliced into strips
- Sugar, 1 tsp.
- Cucumber, 1, julienned

For the Dressing:

- Japanese rice vinegar, 3 tbsp. Or Soy sauce, 2 tbsp.

For Topping:
- Nori strips
- Karashi mustard
- Red pickled ginger
- Roasted white sesame seeds

Procedure:

Combine sugar with eggs and add ¼ of this mixture into a pan and fry into crepes. Make 4 crepes.

Allow egg crepes to cool a little then cut it into long strips.

Prepare noodles according to the package directions. Drain and rinse.

Divide cooked noodles among four serving bowls and top it with egg strips, chicken, and cucumber.

Drizzle rice vinegar and garnish with red pickled ginger, seaweed, roasted sesame seeds and mustard.

17) Sesame-Crusted Tuna With Ponzu Glaze On Ramen Noodles

This recipe is a great illusion of a fancy dish and may appear intimidating to some. However, this is simply an easy work of creativity and is ready in no time. If you are looking for something to impress your guests and be praised then this dish is the perfect pick.

Serving Sizes: **2**

Cooking Time: **15 minutes**

List of Ingredients:

- Ramen noodles, 1 package
- Ponzu sauce, ¼ cup
- Tuna steaks, 2, about 1 inch thick
- Vegetable oil, 2 tsp.
- Honey, 2 tbsp.
- Sesame seeds, ½ cup

- Scallions, 2, thinly sliced
- Sesame oil, 2 tsp., divided

Procedure:

Combine ponzu sauce with 1 tsp. sesame oil, honey and white parts of scallions. Coat tuna steaks well in this marinade and keep aside for 10 minutes.

Coat marinated tuna steaks with sesame seeds evenly.

Heat vegetable oil and cook steaks for 6 minutes. Transfer to a large bowl and cover with aluminum.

In the same pan add the reserved marinade and stir continuously until it thickens.

Cook noodles in for 3 minutes in boiling water. Drain and rinse well.

Put it back in the pot and add 1 tsp. of sesame oil. Toss well.

Divide noodles among two serving plates and place tuna on top. Pour the glaze and top it with greens.

Serve immediately.

18) Abura Soba Noodles

The topping of abura soba noodles can vary according to your taste. This recipe features the basic topping but you can also add additional condiments like cabbage, pork char siu, boiled egg, bean sprout or chicken pieces.

Serving Sizes: **1**

Cooking Time: **10 minutes**

List of Ingredients:

- Soba noodles, 1 package
- Vinegar, 1 tsp.
- Dashi stock granules, 1/3 tsp.
- Oyster sauce, 1 tbsp.
- Green jalapeno sauce, 1 tbsp.
- Sugar, ½ tsp.
- Red onion, ½ sliced
- Nori, 1 sheet, thinly sliced

- Scallions, handful, sliced
- Soy sauce, 1 tbsp.
- Sesame seeds, 1 tsp.
- Pickled red ginger, to taste
- Red pepper flakes, to taste
- Sesame oil, 1 tsp.
- Wei pa/ chicken soup stock granules, ½ tsp.
- Water, 1 tbsp.
- La-yu chili oil, to taste
- XO sauce, 1/3 tsp. (optional)
- Lard, 1 tsp.

Procedure:

Fill a pot with water and boil noodles. Keep aside.

In a medium bowl combine all the ingredients together. Whisk thoroughly so that no lumps remain.

Now toss soba noodles in the prepared dressing.

Garnish with pickled red ginger and red pepper flakes. Drizzle chili oil and serve.

19) Ramen Noodle Salad With Zucchini And Carrots

Summer is just around the corner and it is very difficult to spend long hours in the kitchen, especially during afternoon. This salad recipe with noodles is ready in seconds but if you have time then it is recommended that you allow it cool in the refrigerator for a few hours and then serve.

Serving Sizes: **8**

Cooking Time: **10 minutes**

List of Ingredients:
- Soy sauce, ¼ cup
- Ramen noodles, 4 packages, chili flavor
- Lime juice from 3 limes
- Vegetable oil, 2 tbsp.
- Honey, 2 tsp.

- Ginger, 1 tbsp., minced
- Sesame seeds, 1 tbsp.
- Carrots, 4, peeled and sliced into thin matchsticks
- Scallions, 2, sliced diagonally
- Zucchini, 2, sliced into matchsticks

Procedure:

Combine soy sauce with ½ tsp. of seasoning mix, lime juice, oil, soy sauce, honey and ginger. Mix well and keep aside.

Put a pot filled with water on boil and add noodles. Cook for 3 minutes. Drain and rinse. Allow it to cool completely.

Now mix noodles with veggies in bowl. Drizzle the dressing and toss well.

Add sesame seeds and refrigerate for at least 2-3 hours

Serve.

20) Ramen And Cheese

Who doesn't like mac and cheese? This recipe is a Japanese interpretation of mac and cheese. It is super quick and easy. This entire recipe requires 2 ingredients and you are good to go. Ramen and cheese are great for times when you are avoiding long hours in the kitchen and want to eat something light.

Serving Sizes: **1**

Cooking Time: **8 minutes**

List of Ingredients:
- Velveeta cheese, 2/3 piece
- Ramen noodles, 1 package, chicken flavored

Procedure:

Break noodles into small pieces and put in a saucepan filled with water. Boil for a few minutes until the noodles are tender.

Transfer cooked noodles to a microwavable bowl and top it with cheese. Heat in the microwave for a few seconds to allow it to melt.

Serve.

21) Ramen Noodles With Wild Mushrooms And Parmesan Sauce

This recipe makes a creamy and flavorful Alfredo-like sauce tossed with tender ramen noodles and juicy mushrooms. You can use any variety of mushrooms in this recipe or you can use a combination of different mushrooms together.

Serving Sizes: **4**
Cooking Time: **15 minutes**

List of Ingredients:

- Wild mushrooms, 6 oz. steamed and sliced
- Ramen noodles, 2 packages, any flavor
- Unsalted butter, 2 tbsp.
- Milk, 1 ½ cups
- Salt, to taste
- Ground nutmeg, 1/8 tsp.
- Pepper, to taste
- Flour, 2 tbsp.
- Parmesan cheese, ½ cup, grated
- Extra-virgin olive oil, 1 tbsp.

Procedure:

Heat oil over medium heat and sauté mushrooms for 10 minutes.

Season with pepper and salt and transfer to a bowl. Wrap with plastic or aluminum and keep aside.

Melt butter in a saucepan and add flour. Whisk until a smooth paste forms. Add milk and keep whisking to avoid any lumps. When there are no lumps increase the heat a little and simmer for 8 minutes while stirring occasionally.

Add nutmeg and parmesan and cook for 5 minutes.

Fill a pot with water and add ramen noodles. Do not add the seasoning mix. Boil the noodles for 3 minutes. Drain well.

Add noodles to the sauce and combine well.

Divide noodles in individual serving bowls and top with mushrooms and cheese.

22) Tom Yum Noodle Soup

This recipe is a spicy blend of flavors and perfect for those who like extra heat. You can also use pork meat or chicken with the seafood. This soup has tangy and fiery flavors and a single bowl is enough to keep you full for hours.

Serving Sizes: **2**

Cooking Time: **15 minutes**

List of Ingredients:
- Soba/chukamen noodles, 1 package
- Shrimps, 6, shelled and deveined
- Lime juice, 1 ½ tbsp.
- Galangal, 4 slices
- Chili powder, 3 dashes

- Water, 1 ¼ cups
- Small tomato, ½ cut into wedges
- Canned Oyster mushrooms, 6, halved
- Fish sauce, ½ tbsp.
- Lemongrass, 1 stalk, white part bruised and pounded
- Kaffir lime leaves, 5, bruised
- Roasted chili paste, 1 ½ tbsp.
- Cilantro, for garnish

Procedure:

Cook noodles according to the directions printed at the back of the package. Drain and place in a serving bowl.

Fill a stock pot with water and bring it to a boil. Add all the ingredients in the boiling water except chili powder, lime juice and fish sauce. Cook until the shrimps are done.

Now stir fish sauce and season with chili powder. Stir well.

Lastly add lime juice and stir once.

Ladle the soup over cooked noodles and garnish with cilantro.

Serve.

23) Salmon In Parchment

This is a healthy recipe featuring a combination of salmon and ramen noodles. The flaky salmon fillets are cooked in the heat and in their own juices absorbing the flavors from the vegetables. The flavors are balanced and perfect for those who avoid spicy food.

Serving Sizes: **4**

Cooking Time: **20 minutes**

List of Ingredients:
- Ramen noodles, 8 oz.
- Salmon fillet, 24 oz. cut into 4 pieces
- Fresh dill, 2 tbsp.
- Asparagus tips, 1 cup
- Dijon mustard, 2 tbsp.
- Salt, ¼ tsp.
- Large sheets of parchment paper, 4
- Carrots, 1 cup, julienned

- Red bell pepper, 1 cup, julienned
- Extra-virgin olive oil, 1 tbsp.
- Zucchini, 1 cup, julienned

Procedure:

Preheat the oven to 400 F.

Cooking ramen noodles in boiling water until al dente. Rinse and drain. Drizzle some oil and sprinkle with dill and salt. Keep aside.

Rub Dijon mustard over the salmon fillets evenly.

Fold parchment paper in half and cut it into a half heart. Open the shape and place ¼ noodles in the middle of the heart then top it with salmon fillet and vegetables. Fold the edges and enclose tightly.

Arrange the parchment pouches on the rack and bake for 10 minutes.

Serve hot.

24) Ramepherd's Pie

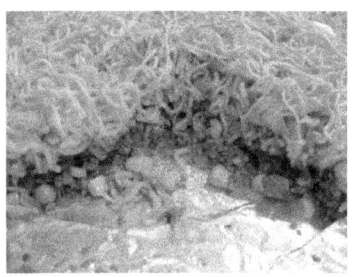

This recipe is a delicious reproduction of shepherd's pie made with beef flavored ramen noodles. Instead of mashed potatoes as a base, ramepherd's pie uses beef mince, onion and peas with a crispy topping of ramen noodles.

Serving Sizes: **2**

Cooking Time: **10 minutes**

List of Ingredients:
- Beef flavored ramen noodles, 1 package
- Ground beef, ½ pound
- Frozen peas, ½ cup
- Vegetable oil, 2 tsp.
- Salt, to taste
- Pepper, to taste
- Onion, ½ cup, chopped
- Water, ¼ cup

- Vegetable oil, 2 tsp.
- Worcestershire sauce, 2 tsp.

Procedure:

Fill a pot with water and boil noodles until done. Drain and keep aside.

Heat oil in a pan and cook beef. Use a wooden spoon to crumble the meat and cook until it is no longer pink.

Stir water and add peas, sauce and onions.

Season with salt and pepper.

Transfer the mixture into a large dish and spread noodles over it.

Broil for 10 minutes or until crispy and turns brown in color.

25) Stir-Fry Ramen With Peppers And Shrimp

This recipe is known as Ebi Yakasobe in Japanese. It is a quick stir fry recipe made with simple ingredients. The flavors are both spicy and savory. You can add more veggies of your choice to this stir-fry recipe.

Serving Sizes: **4**

Cooking Time: **15 minutes**

List of Ingredients:

- Shrimp-flavored ramen noodles, 6 oz.
- Cooked shrimps, 12 oz. tails removed
- Fresh pea pods, ¾ cup, strings and tips removed
- Bok choy, 2 cups, chopped
- Sweet yellow pepper, 1 medium, slice into thin strips
- Green onion, 1/3 cup, sliced
- Toasted sesame oil, 2 tsp.

- Cooking oil, 1 tbsp.
- Sesame seeds, 2 tsp., toasted
- Orange juice, ¼ cup
- Hoisin sauce, ¼ cup
- Crushed red pepper flakes, ¼ tsp.

Procedure:

Prepare noodles according to the directions printed on the package. Drain well.

Add toasted sesame oil to a pan and add noodles. Toss well and cook for 5 minutes. Keep aside.

Heat cooking oil and stir-fry sweet pepper for 2 minutes then stir fry bok choy and pea pod for another 2 minutes.

Add green onions and shrimp. Season with crushed pepper, orange juice and hoisin sauce. Combine well and stir fry for 3 minutes.

Divide cooked noodles on serving plates and top it with the shrimp mixture. Dust sesame seeds and enjoy.

26) Crunchy Ramen Snack Mix

This recipe makes a healthy snack for you to munch on during odd times of the day and is a unique way to put ramen noodles to use. This recipe is also very different from the categorized soups and stir-fry's that are usually made with noodles.

Serving Sizes: **2**

Cooking Time: **10 minutes**

List of Ingredients:

- Ramen noodles, 2 packages, broken into small pieces
- Cornflakes, 1 cup
- Cayenne pepper, ½ tsp.
- Raw cashews, 1 cup
- Curry powder, 4 tsp.
- Raw peanuts, 1 cup
- Dried wasabi peas, ½ cup
- Vegetable oil, 3 tbsp.
- Salt, ½ tsp.

Procedure:

Preheat the oven to 400F.

Arrange individual layers of peanuts, cashews, cornflakes and ramen on a rimmed baking sheet.

Drizzle oil and coat the contents well.

Sprinkle curry powder, salt and cayenne pepper.

Pop the sheet in the oven and bake for 10 minutes while stirring twice while baking.

Top it wasabi peas and allow it to cool.

Serve.

27) Ramen Burger

This recipe adds a noodle twist to the burgers and is very different from what you typically eat. This recipe uses ramen noodles at the top and bottom base in place of burger buns. Your noodles should be crispy and crunchy to achieve the perfect texture of a burger bun. You can stuff your burgers with any kind of filling you like.

Serving Sizes: **2**

Cooking Time: **20 minutes**

List of Ingredients:
- Ramen noodles, 1 pack
- Vegetable oil, 2 tbsp.
- Cheddar cheese, 2 slices
- Ground beef patties, 2
- Tomato, 1, sliced into round shape
- Onion, ½, sliced into round shape

- Ground black pepper, to taste
- Salt, to taste

Procedure:

Prepare noodles according to the direction printed on the package. Drain thoroughly and spread them on a rimmed baking sheet. Sprinkle salt and pepper.

Use a small ring mold or any can of 28 oz. and scoop out four round piles of noodle.

Heat oil in a large pan and fry noodles until each side turns brown. Transfer on paper towel.

Season beef patties with salt, seasoning mix and pepper. Cook in the same pan for 2 minutes on each side. Now place a cheese slice on each patty keep cooking until done.

Now place patties on each noodle bun add ring shaped onions, tomatoes and another noodle bun to cover.

Serve.

28) Salmon Cakes With Creamy Tomato-Garlic Sauce

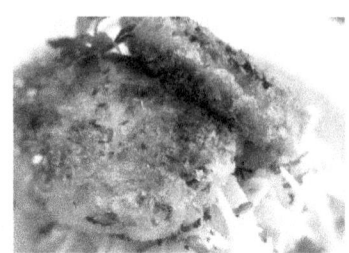

This recipe makes 8 mini salmon burger cakes. Once in a while it is good to skip typical beef and chicken burgers and try something different for a change. You can also eat these salmon cakes without patties as a snack. The addition of noodles makes this dish a delicacy.

Serving Sizes: **8**

Cooking Time: **15 minutes**

List of Ingredients:

- Fresh ramen noodles, 1 package, broken into small pieces
- Pink salmon, 1 can of 418 g, drained
- Olive oil, 1 tbsp.
- Dried breadcrumbs, 2 tbsp. + ½ cup
- Garlic, 2 cloves, peeled
- Capers, 1 tbsp., thoroughly rinsed and drained

- Large baking potato, 1, thinly sliced
- Fresh dill, ½ cup, chopped

For the Sauce:

- Garlic, 2 cloves, peeled
- Hot chili sauce, ½ tsp.
- Sundried tomatoes, ¼ cup (not oil-packed)
- Plain yogurt, 100 g

Procedure:

For sauce put a small pot on heat filled with water. Add garlic and sundried tomatoes and for 3 minutes. Drain the mixture and reserve 1/3 cup of the mixture.

Process tomatoes and garlic mixture with yogurt, reserved mixture and chili sauce in a blender until smooth. Transfer to a serving sauce bowl and keep aside.

Fill another pot with water and add garlic and potatoes. Boil until potatoes are fork tender. Drain and transfer potatoes and garlic in a bowl and using a potato masher, mash it finely.

Meanwhile potatoes are boiling prepare noodles according to the directions.

Add dill, salmon, noodles, capers and 2 tbsp. of breadcrumbs. Incorporate everything well.

Take spoonful of the mixture at a time and form 8 cakes. Coat each cake in the remaining breadcrumbs.

Heat oil in a nonstick pan and fry salmon cakes until each side turns golden brown.

Transfer to paper towel to drain excess oil.

Serve with hot tomato garlic sauce.

29) Ramen Crust Pizza

This is a unique pizza recipe is made solely from chewy and crispy ramen noodles. You can use whatever you like as your topping like mushrooms, pepperoni, olives, jalapeno, bell peppers, scallions, chicken chunks, roasted pepper or sausages.

Serving Sizes: **3**

Cooking Time: **30 minutes**

List of Ingredients:

- Ramen noodles, 2 packages
- Parmesan cheese, 2 ounces, grated
- Extra-virgin olive oil, 3 tbsp.
- Pizza sauce, 3/4 cup
- Mozzarella, 12 ounces, grated

Procedure:

Preheat the oven to 450 F.

Break noodles into medium size piece and cook in a boiling salted water for 2 minutes. DONOT add the seasoning mix at all. Drain and keep aside.

Heat oil in a large pan and add noodles covering the pan completely. Keep the heat low.

Spread 6 oz. mozzarella over the noodles followed by pizza sauce. Again spread the remaining mozzarella and half parmesan, make an even layer.

Top with olives, pepperoni and jalapeno. Pop the dish in the oven and bake for 20 minutes.

Spread remaining parmesan. When the pizza cools down a little use a spatula to loosen the edges. Slice and serve hot.

30) Ramen-Crusted Fried Chicken

This recipe makes juicy and spicy chicken wings coated in crunchy and crispy ramen noodles. These crispy chicken wings make a perfect appetizer. If you are unable to marinate the chicken thighs overnight then marinate it for at least 4 hours.

Serving Sizes: **4**

Cooking Time: **25 minutes**

List of Ingredients:
- Chicken flavored ramen noodles, 2 packages

- Cabbage, 2 cups, shredded
- Soy sauce, 2 tbsp.
- Peanut oil, 2 quarts
- Buttermilk, 1 cup
- Chicken thighs with bones, 6 pieces
- Lemon, 1, cut into wedges

Procedure:

Preheat the oven to 30 F.

Combine buttermilk with soy sauce and 1 seasoning packet. Transfer the marinade to a Ziploc bag and add chicken pieces. Coat the meat well in the marinade and seal tightly. Refrigerate overnight.

Break noodles into ¼ inch pieces and process about ¾ of the noodles in a blender.

Add both noodles and processed noodle meal in a bowl and coat each marinated chicken piece in this mixture.

Heat oil in a large pan and fry wings until each side turns nice golden brown.

Arrange the fried wings on a rimmed baking sheet and bake for 10 minutes.

Transfer baked chicken thighs on a serving platter and sprinkle with a dash of seasoning mix.

Serve with lemon wedges and cabbage.

Healthy Ramen Noodles

Sweet Potato Ramen

Ingredients:

- 1 T sesame oil
- 1 tsp minced garlic
- 2 tsp grated ginger
- 4 C vegetable broth
- 4 C water
- 2 C canned mushrooms, sliced
- 1 C frozen corn
- 1 head bok choy, sliced, thinly
- 3 carrots, sliced
- 1 lbs. sweet potatoes, cooked and cubed
- 3 oz. ramen noodles, crushed
- 4 scallions, sliced
- 2 T hot sauce
- 2 T fresh cilantro, chopped
- Salt and pepper to taste

Directions:

1. Heat your oil and sauté ginger and garlic slowly add in vegetable broth with your water.
2. Let simmer for a few minutes adding in everything but your scallions.
3. Let noodles cook, let veggies get tender
4. Add hot sauce and scallions last

5. Garnish to taste

Hot Garlic Ramen

Ingredients:
- 2 T sesame oil
- 4 scallions, diced
- 3 T minced garlic
- ½ tsp ginger, ground
- 4 C water
- 3 ½ t sweet white
- 2 T soy sauce
- 1 lbs. chicken breast, cooked and sliced or cubed
- 8 C baby spinach
- 1 package ramen noodles
- 1 white onion, diced
- 2 C sliced mushrooms
- ½ tsp crushed red pepper flakes
- 2 tsp. basil, chopped
- Salt and pepper to taste

Directions:
1. Heat saucepan with your oil and sauté your ginger, scallions and garlic heat for about 2 minutes
2. Cook for a few minutes and add remaining ingredients, stirring in ramen noodles and cooked chicken, bringing to a boil

3. Stir and heat until chicken is tender and falling apart
4. Serve

www.ingramcontent.com/pod-product-compliance
Lightning Source LLC
Chambersburg PA
CBHW071440070526
44578CB00001B/169